SKIING WITH KIDS

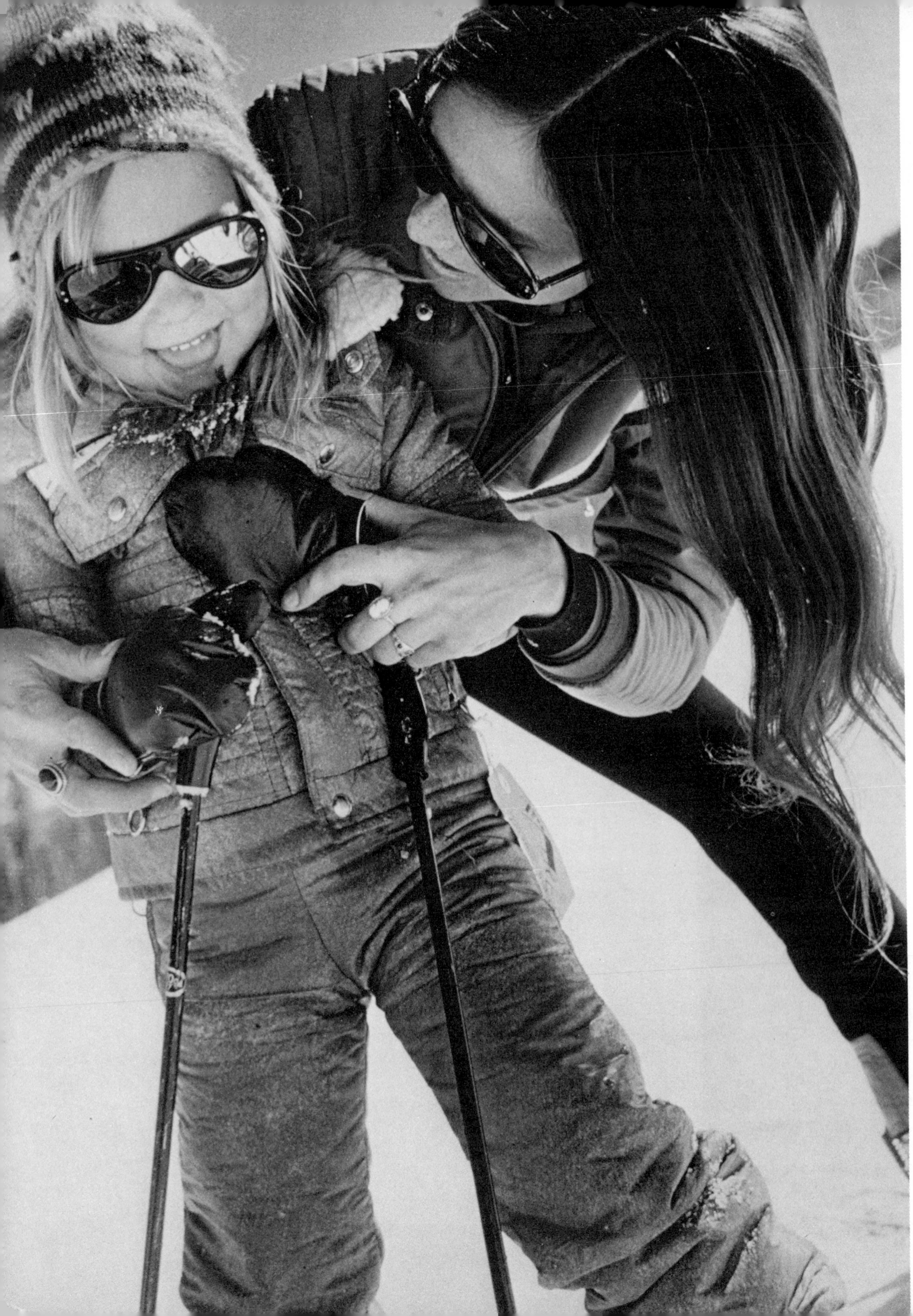

Vail photo by Peter Runyon

Skiing with Kids

by Christi Mueller Northrop

THE CHATHAM PRESS, OLD GREENWICH, CONNECTICUT

ACKNOWLEDGMENTS

My special thanks and appreciation to those fine people who gave me so much help and encouragement.

Rudi Mattesich
Sue Bromley
Dale Bromley
Kyle van Saun
Mike Grab
Ellen Begleiter

I also thank the ski areas I visited, the areas that provided me with information and pictures, and the many helpful manufacturers. I especially thank the following very cooperative, friendly people.

Hadley Gray
Nancy Alfara
Micky and Ernie Blake
Junior Bounous
Muriel Bouton
Ronnie Connley
Peter Dahl
George Engle
Sepp Froehlich
Hans Garger
Lynn Jones
Dixi Nohl
Stu Parks
Paul Pfosi
Peter Runyon
Ruthie Rowley
David Stewart

DEDICATION

To the skiing Moms and Dads especially Ned, Retty and Willi and the skiing kids, especially Will and Kitty

Library of Congress Catalog Card Number: 76-18486
ISBN: 0-85699-136-8

Printed in the United States of America

CONTENTS

Foreword

As I searched the muddy, ski boot-trodden floor by the candy machine for the ski glove from Santa, I began to wonder if skiing with children was really worth the painstaking effort and endless patience required. Yet, I couldn't help but remember the excitement and pride exhibited by my five-year-old son when he had successfully snowplowed down the hill without falling. With his pleas for "just one more run, Mom," I realized that he too was bitten by the ski bug. What was one lost mitten? My son and I really had something more to share.

Skiing with children can be so rewarding; an experience the whole family can enjoy together. In spite of soggy mittens, mislaid gear, broken bindings, runny noses, and cold feet, there are great compensations such as that perfect day dreamed of by every skier, young and old, right off the page of the Swiss calendar in the kitchen. And afterward, when a rosy-cheeked, freckled-nosed child looks up at you over his hot chocolate and says, "Gee, that was great! Thanks for taking me," you know it was all worthwhile.

In contrast to many sports such as swimming, for instance, skiing is somewhat unnatural. Being a man-made sport, a lot of mechanical equipment is needed to fool mother nature and make it all possible. Along with this necessary special equipment, comes a great potential for problems for all of us, including, and especially, our children. Yet, if we can master the mountains, we can also manage the mechanical and organizational chores that can seem to darken any morning prior to a day on the slopes.

It is my intention to help parents of young skiers by paving the way for that perfect day

The author's family at Steamboat; photo by Christi Northrop

and can best describe this book as a guide to avoiding the hassles and frustrations of skiing with children. I do not intend to include every aspect of skiing in this book since there are too many complex techniques and differences of opinion about them that could obscure the main objective. Also, there are many opinions concerning dealing with children. My recommendations and procedures are based on personal experience and, while I do not maintain that this is the only way, I hope that parents can benefit from what I have learned.

I thank all the skiing families that have helped me by offering advice from their experiences and I also appreciate the assistance and information provided by the many ski areas, shops, and individuals especially involved in the ski industry.

—Christi Mueller Northrop

1 Is Your Child Ready to Ski?

Growing up in Colorado with Winter Park ski area in our backyard, we started skiing at a very early age. It is hard to remember actually learning to ski or having any fears except the T-bar that became a chair lift for us. In fact, skiing was a natural pasttime, like going to the park to play.

Young children take to skiing very easily and naturally if properly taught. For them, learning this sport is no different than learning to ride a bike, a horse, or to swim, except that it usually involves a longer ride in the car. As with any new experience, skiing should be approached and explained very carefully.

One of the most important questions every parent should ask is: "Is the child really ready and *eager* to learn to ski?" With younger children, this is hard to determine and sometimes cannot be answered until it has actually been tried. If children are anxious to ski and have heard how much fun it is from friends and family, there should be no problem introducing them to the sport. Also, it is helpful if they enjoy physical activity and the learning of new sports in general. None too obvious is the fact that the child should enjoy being outdoors in winter. When children dislike snow and cold, it should also be obvious that it is usually because they are not properly dressed.

Some other very basic points parents should consider are, whether the child has the physical coordination to handle skis, and whether he is in good enough physical shape to tackle a sport that demands strong control over his body movements. Also, is the child mature enough to handle the newness and strangeness of this sport? Is he able to cope with the difficulties and frustrations which might result from learning to ski? Can the child follow and obey instructions well? Think how many instructions are required to get a child from the parking lot to the base lodge, much less actually learn to ski and deal with his equipment.

There are no two children alike; as parents well know, each child is an individual and thus, will react to skiing differently. From my experience, I find that children are ready to ski at varying ages: one may be ready or willing at as young an age as two and a half or three years, while a brother or sister in the same family may not really be ready to ski until ten. If the reluctant child is forced to ski, he may never enjoy the sport, though, some stubborn children may respond to special coaxing from parents. Coaxing and encouraging a child is far different from forcing him and these stubborn children often enjoy skiing inspite of themselves.

In the last few years, we have seen more and more very young children skiing. The manufacturers are now offering outfits and equipment for children as young as two, while ski magazines and area brochures are pictorially encouraging skiing for very small children. I feel that this publicity and surge of interest in toddler skiing sometimes falsely encourages parents to introduce the sport to young children too soon. For some young pre-schoolers, just the experience of taking a day trip to a mountain and being placed in a strange nursery with other unfamiliar children is all they can possibly handle. To add to this the physical problems for a toddler on the slopes and all the other attendant emotional experiences is frequently asking far too much.

Some parents feel guilty about going skiing and leaving a young child in the nursery all day. They then rent equipment for an hour or two and take the child directly up the lift to ski down between their knees. They just want the child to get the "feeling of skiing". This is not benefiting anyone. The child, with no proper introduction to skiing, can find the lift and trip down, even between Dad's legs, very frightening. Parents would do better to use the same time to build a snowman or just let the child play in the snow. Unless a two and a half or three-year-old has many opportunities to ski during the season, he will not profit much from being placed on skis once or twice during the winter. These tiny children we see racing down courses in film clips or in magazines are usually the sons or daughters of ski instructors or ski area personnel. With so much opportunity to ski and so much exposure, they should not be compared with the average young child whose experience is limited to weekends and holidays.

I feel it is better to wait until the child is four or five and can really begin to understand what skiing is all about. All of this depends upon the individual child; a four year old weekend or holiday skier can actually learn a lot and begin to control those wobbly legs, heavy boots, and awkward skis. However, I personally have found five is the magic age for learning. A five-year-old is now familiar with group experiences and very often is in kindergarten where he is used to following directions and paying attention to a teacher. It is not unusual to see a child of this age progress from a first-time beginner to a mountain mogul skier in one season. It is amazing how quickly most five-year-olds learn. In summary:

Two and a half - four years: *introduction to skiing with emphasis on fun and games*
Five - twelve years: *organized ski instruction with emphasis on actually mastering techniques and skills.*

From time to time, one sees a parent skiing with a small child on his back in a pack rig or kiddie carrier. I have heard these parents propose the notion that this will help the child get a feel for skiing at an early, early age and therefore, skiing will become more natural to him. Skiing with children in a backpack is not very advantageous to them and, in fact can be very dangerous. When you are Alpine skiing, you are often traveling at a fairly fast rate. The hazards for a small child if the parent fell or was hit by another skier should be obvious. Riding the chair lift with the pack rig is another extremely difficult feat, as the parent must take the child off his back, and somehow manage everything, poles, backpack, and child.

However, taking a child out on a cross-country ski tour when he is on his parent's back is a far different matter. If the infant is properly dressed and plenty of extra food, snacks, juice, and bottles are brought along, there is no reason why a young child cannot accompany his parents. Extra concern should be given to the weather and the length of the tour. The parents should know the exact trail when taking a small child along. It is very important that a parent, setting out on such a ski tour with a young child on his back, be sure that he himself is in good condition and that there is another adult able to spell him or take over if unforeseen problems arise. Even a young child, all bundled in his winter clothes, can get very heavy after an hour.

Whether or not the parent is ready for the whole scene is an equally important matter. Patience, patience, patience — no parent can have enough. If you are going to ski with children, you have to realize that it is going to take much more time and effort than if you were skiing on your own or with a group of adults.

Whether a parent is dealing with a junior racer, a young freestyler, a Nordic competitor, or a toddler beginner, patience is equally important on all levels. It is just as essential that the older, more advanced child, who may be competing, does not sense his parents' impatience and feel an added pressure on him to succeed. When parents push their children to accomplish too much too fast on all levels, chances of injury are greatly increased. Under pressure the child has a tendency to tense up in the effort to push himself. Most children are naturally relaxed and resilient and this natural spontaneity and ability to adapt should be capitalized upon when introducing the child to skiing.

Again, only you, the parent, can decide whether your child is ready to ski. For older children, it should be a joint decision. In fact, many children have talked their parents into taking up the sport from the encouragement of peers at school who are avid skiers. But parents beware — if you are all learning at the same time, don't get discouraged if, on the third or fourth day, your son is riding the lift and skiing down over the bumps while you are still on the "bunny hill". Children learn quickly. They do not have the same fears of speed, falling, and of adapting to new environments that we adults often have. They do not have quite the same feeling that they are making fools of themselves and are generally less self-conscious when learning a new sport. This enables them to relax and respond naturally. If Dad or Mom has had one or two lessons and then decides it's time to introduce the child to skiing, please don't try to pass on the information you have learned from your limited skiing experience. Let the instructor or the ski school teach your child to ski while you yourself concentrate on learning. Frequently adults are taught in a different method than children.

Getting ready to go skiing can often be the biggest hassle of all. Families, who have had ample experience skiing with their children have, over a period of many years, undoubtedly learned how to organize themselves through trial and error with many tales of woe and trauma. Eventually they decide who is responsible for what equipment, where the mittens are, etc. Careful planning helps avoid the chaos. Organization and preparation the night before a family departs for skiing is essential and can make or break the next day. It is helpful if each child has a bag or knapsack with his own gear for which he is responsible. If you watch families getting out of their cars in a ski area parking lot, it doesn't take long to determine which are organized and off to a good day and which are never going to survive without mass confusion.

Skiing families should always be sure to test the adjustment of car ski racks if they plan to use them for children's skis as well. Many children's skis easily fit in the trunk. However, it is important to see that the front and back parts of the car rack are close enough to accommodate short children's skis. There is nothing worse than having to readjust racks early in the morning. Also, always double check that all rack closings are tightly secured especially if children are loading their own skis.

Checking with friends who have skied with their children can prove helpful. Ask for advice concerning local ski areas and local ski shops. However, consider the advice carefully. One family's bad experience at a particular area should not completely rule out that area. So much depends upon personalities, ages, weather, and snow conditions. Take skiing advice just as you would any other neighborly advice. It can often prove helpful but also sometimes be misleading.

Once you decide your child is ready to ski, it is important to remember that skiing is a sport, a recreation, something freely chosen for enjoyment. It should be FUN and children should look forward to it. After all, it is a pasttime that is exciting, invigorating, and just plain terrific. Skiing should never be a "boot camp" experience. The sport provides a chance for families to be outdoors and enjoy the natural beauties of our winter environment. You and I, as parents, welcome a day in the snow, hopefully the sun, and those crisp, cool mountain breezes to maintain our peace of mind just as much as a child needs the experience for developmental purposes. As skiing becomes more commercial and stylish, we often forget the purely recreational aspect of the sport. Once a family experiences a great day gliding through the trees on a lovely Nordic tour, or whizzing down the slopes in and out of moguls or over beautifully smooth, groomed trails, it is hard not to become a family of ski fanatics. Children can be as rapidly bitten by the "ski bug" as adults.

There is one last question I have often been asked which, perhaps, is the earliest concern in skiing with kids. Should a mother ski while she is pregnant? This question can only be answered by the woman's obstetrician, though there are several schools of thought on this issue and a lot depends upon the doctor's familiarity with the sport. So much also depends upon the mother's physical condition and if she has been skiing all along. A pregnant mother should also ask her doctor how long he would permit her to ski and about skiing at high altitudes. If the doctor does give her the okay, it should be unnecessary to suggest that she take plenty of rest and doesn't push it. There will always be another season. Also, avoid slopes that are especially popular with the "hot dog" skiers and be wary of any congested area where the chances of being hit, probably the greatest danger, are increased.

Photo courtesy of Sun Valley

II   Clothing

You've decided that your child is ready and willing to ski, and that you, as a parent, have the necessary patience. Now that the Halloween pumpkins are in the garbage cans and Christmas is not far away, our minds turn reluctantly to Santa's ever-shrinking sled, perhaps in terms of ski gear. Clothing seems to come to mind first, since we can't rent long underwear or ski pants. The ski industry in the U.S. is ever expanding, especially in the area of children's equipment. Yet, like fashion in general, brands, styles and manufacturers are constantly changing. Each season new materials, designs, and colors are available, giving parents a much larger selection to choose from. Price, quality, fit, and the opportunities to use the article for more than one season or hand it down to a younger sibling should be of greater concern to parents than brand names.

Unfortunately, few of us live in areas that have a special, children's ski shop. These do exist but, alas, are few and far between. Usually we are confined to looking in a small corner of a general ski shop and plowing through crowded racks in search of that pair of size 6, red, warmup pants, while on the other side of the ski shop, the men's and ladies' outfits are beautifully displayed on wide, accessible racks. Some department stores also carry ski clothing for children but it is best to check with a ski shop first to see what is available, and then perhaps compare the selections. The ski shops usually do carry the best available stock. I have listed brand names of clothing in this chapter which will hopefully assist parents in shopping. Most of these brands are marketed throughout the country. Also, these selected manufacturers seem to have paid careful attention to children's needs. I have not included expensive import lines or clothing designed specifically for racers. There are probably other brands that your shop carries which I have omitted. These brands could prove perfectly adequate, but again, check for quality and fit.

Ski clothing should keep a child warm, dry, and protected from the wind and at the same time allow for maximum activity and movement. Children get cold and lose body heat much faster than adults. Good, winter ski clothing helps retain this natural warmth and several layers are most effective in trapping it by forming insulating air pockets between the layers. Forget the style. If the child is uncomfortable and cannot move well, the particular article will not be adequate. The outer layers must be relatively easy to put on and take off and well designed so those cold, little fingers can manage on their own. This is where good wide zippers and easy snaps play an important role. It is also helpful to know that the bright colors are more than pretty; they help both the parent and other skiers on the hill spot the children. If a small child is snowplowing down a cat walk and is brightly dressed, he can be more readily seen by those coming down behind him. At least for the parent's sake, all ski clothing should be well marked with name tags. The tags can also assist the child in identifying his own belongings, and help the ski school send the right parka home with the right child.

Before I describe the individual garments, I should first mention the various materials used in ski clothing. A fabric or material is not warm in and of itself; it is "warm" because of its ability to trap and retain body heat. Wool has always been noted and hardly matched for its marvelous ability in this regard. Yet, new synthetics have been developed which are ideal for skiing. Each season, we find parkas and ski pants bearing labels describing new materials and new ways of processing materials that will make these articles especially warm and resistant to wind and water. The use of synthetics has been especially important because it is now possible for ski wear to be lightweight, very flexible and yet extremely warm and durable. In the course of looking for children's parkas and pants, parents will undoubtedly come across such words as Antron, Nysilk and Taslon. In addition, sweaters are also often knit from acrylics and parkas are filled with Dacron Fiberfill or a synthetic down known as Polarguard. Most, happily, are machine washable. There are two other important terms parents should look for. One is "anti-glisse", which merely means that the material is textured in such a way that the child is less apt to slide great distances on the snow when he falls. The other important term to look for is ZePel, a process of treating the material to make it more stain and water resistant. Various chemical companies may have a similar process with different names. ZePel helps keep light-colored ski clothing clean. No matter which fabric the article of ski clothing is made out of, parents should still carefully check for the construction and quality of workmanship and not overlook the natural fabrics: wool, cotton, and goose or duck down. These materials have long been proven and acclaimed.

LONG UNDERWEAR

Specially constructed thermal or insulated long underwear helps trap body heat, is soft next to the skin, and stretches and gives well with movement. Waist, neck, and cuffs should not be too tight and binding. I feel wool right next to the skin should be avoided since it can be too itchy for children.

Long underwear can be purchased with separate tops and bottoms or as a one-piece suit. I feel the two-piece suits are easier for frequent bathroom stops. Cotton knit pajamas (without feet) can be substituted if they fit snuggly. Some long underwear can be multi-purpose to serve as pajamas, or even substitute for a jersey since it has a finished look and is made from a nicer fabric. Heavier knit tights can also be used, but be sure the foot fits smoothly and is not too tight. Too many seams in the foot can be uncomfortable with boot pressure. Short sleeve regular T-shirts are adequate substitute tops unless temperatures are apt to be very low.

Suggested Manufacturers:
   Allen - A
   Sears Roebuck (size 2 - 20)
   Duofold (size 6 - 14)
   Little Johns (size 4 - 14)
Cost range: $4.00 - $15.00 per set

SOCKS

Two pairs of socks, one heavy and one light, prove to be best inside ski boots. Three pairs is the absolute maximum. New boots are made with more and better insulation which helps eliminate the need for several sock layers. If the toes can't wiggle, feet will soon be cold. Socks should be long enough to come above the boot tops and fit over the long under-wear cuff. Also, they should fit smoothly with no wrinkles. Sock wrinkles can be easily felt and are highly uncomfortable in a ski boot. The outside pair should be wool or a combina-tion of materials often referred to as thermal. Thermal tube socks are good for children as they fit various foot sizes well. Clean socks fit better and keep the foot warmer. If you have accidently shrunk a pair of your own good, wool socks, these are perfect for your children if they are long enough. Again, adequate socks are probably available already at home.

Suggested Manufacturers:
   Obermeyer
   Wigwam
   Weiss (Beconta)
Cost range: $2.00 - $3.50

T-NECKS

A turtle-neck is worn over a long underwear top. Aside from warmth, T-necks also supply protection for the neck from itchy sweater collars or cold zippers. While most children probably already have perfectly adequate T-necks, ski versions usually have more elastic in the neck and cuffs, and have longer necks. If a child has an ordinary T-neck that is not too stretched out, save your pennies for other equipment.

Suggested Manufacturers:
   Obermeyer
   Skyr
   Hot Gear
Cost range: $5.00 - $10.00

WINDSHIRTS

A windshirt is a thin nylon shirt usually worn over the turtleneck and under the sweater. It provides yet another extra layer and can also be useful as a lightweight wind-breaker on warm days. Windshirts are, by no means, absolutely necessary but can be very helpful at times. They are especially good, and popular, worn over sweaters and under down vests. Not only is this the "in" look, but it is surprisingly warm and comfortable. Most windshirts are very colorful with bright patterns.

Suggested Manufacturers:
   Duffy
   Saska
   Skyr
Cost range: $10.00 - $20.00

SWEATERS

A closely knit, lightweight wool or acrylic sweater keeps the child much warmer than that big bulky sweater that "looks" so warm. If it is very cold, two lightweight sweaters (again creating layers) are warmer than one bulky one. Big heavy sweaters also restrict the child's movement. With a good warm parka, and especially with bib overalls, one light-weight, well-knit sweater is all that is needed. Most likely the child already has such a sweater and doesn't need racing stripes, snowflakes, or reindeer to keep warm. When buying a ski sweater, be sure it is machine washable and that the arms are long enough.

Suggested Manufacturers:
   Demetre
   Hot Gear
   Obermeyer
   Profile
   Meister
Cost range: $12.00 - $30.00

PARKAS

A parka is a warm insulated jacket consisting of two or more layers. Since the torso is one of the most important parts of the body to keep warm, a good parka is of prime im-portance.

The outside shell material is usually a nylon synthetic and it should be strong enough to resist tearing and repell water and wind. If it is a light color, it should be specially treated to be stain resistant. Also, texturized or anti-glisse materials help prevent sliding on the snow. Most parkas are filled with either a synthetic, such as Dacron Fiberfill or Polarguard or with natural goose or duck down. The filling is very important and generally the more filling, the warmer the parka. If down or some synthetics are fluffed up, they form air pockets that trap body heat excellently and are also comfortably lightweight. Hold a parka up to the light to check the amount of filling used and the stitching. The more separate compartments for the down or filling the better, to insure that it will not all slip to the bottom of the jacket.

A good parka is a wise investment as it can often serve as a general winter coat as well.

Parka check list:

1. *Size:* A parka should be roomy enough to fit over several layers of clothing and hopefully allow for growth. The puffier parkas seem to have more grow room than those that are designed to fit closely.

2. *Neck or collar:* The neck should be snug but not binding or irritating. There are many types of collars but I prefer the kind that folds up and can be zipped or snapped. This way the neck and chin can be even more protected on extremely cold days. Certain collars are even filled or padded which is a nice extra. Fur synthetics look warmer than they are; snow easily accumulates on the fur-like material making the chin wet and even colder.

3. *Sleeves and cuffs:* Sleeves should be long and roomy enough to allow for lots of stretching and movement. The cuffs should fit snuggly but not bind. Some manufacturers have storm or snow cuffs inside the sleeve which is a welcome addition; snow should not be able to come up the sleeves. Certain sleeves with Lycra or synthetic stretch panels inserted in the shoulders or arms make moving easy but unless they are "insulated stretch panels", cold air penetrates easily. Most children don't need this racier touch.

4. *Zippers:* If the zipper seems flimsy and hard to work, look for another parka. It is vital that the zipper work freely and smoothly. You would be surprised how many times a day a child zips and unzips it. Two-way zippers are a nice extra but not essential. The very best combination is an inside zipper, a draft flap, and outside snaps. Snaps alone without a zipper, however, leave openings for warmth to escape and wind and snow to get in.

5. *Pockets:* Parka pockets should be accessible from the outside and close securely so nothing is lost. Velcro is great to secure pockets as children need not fiddle with zippers. Again, check the stitching to be sure the pocket is well sewn on. One extra some manufacturers have is a "hand warmer". Children can put their hand in behind the closed pockets from the sides to keep their hands warm without unzipping anything. Be sure there are *enough* pockets.

6. *Hoods:* Several parkas have attached hoods, either insulated or merely a thin shell. These hoods can be a bonanza in a blizzard. When not in use, the hood should be dropped into a small neck pocket and/or lie flat. If it is an insulated hood, it must hang on the back and could, conceivably, be caught on lifts.

7. *Colors:* As mentioned, bright colors are helpful for identifying your child and to in-

crease visibility for other skiers. Choose a parka, however, by its construction and quality first and then by color. If it is a light color, again check for a stain-resisting treatment such as ZePel.

8. *Cleaning:* Practically all children's parkas can be machine-washed. It is important to look for this feature. Down-filled parkas can be put in the dryer with a tennis shoe to prevent the down from becoming matted.

> *Suggested Manufacturers:*
> Aspen
> Alpine Designs
> Beconta
> C.B. Sports
> Edelweiss
> Frostline Kits (you sew it and save costs)
> Gerry
> Hot Gear
> Liberty Bell
> Profile
> Skyr
> Sportscaster
> Swing West
> *Cost range:* $17.00 - $60.00

SKI PANTS

Ski pants are worn over long underwear or in some cases over jeans. Like parkas, it is essential that they are water, wind, stain, and abrasion resistant. It is always good to have warm dry legs but it is not really as essential as a warm torso. If the child is going to ski only a few times and the other expenses are mounting, jeans with a layer or two of long underwear will do. There is a silicone spray on the market called "Raindri" which will help waterproof jeans. If jeans are worn, add gaiters which will help keep the snow out of the boots. There are basically four types or styles of ski pants: stretch pants, insulated, nylon bib-overalls, thin nylon zip or warm-up pants, and knickers.

Stretch pants are usually a combination of wool, nylon, Spandex, Lycra, or other stretch synthetics. They are close fitting but allow for plenty of movement. If the stretch pants have racing stripes or inserted panels of contrasting colors, these, again, should be insulated. Some styles even have padded, bright colored knees — "gate crashers". This is mainly for racing or for style which few young children really need. Be sure the pantleg, if it has a cuff, fits over the top of the boot your child will wear. The foot "stirrup" should be smooth without wrinkles or unnecessary seams. Above all, don't get stretch pants too tight; a child won't be able to bend and will get cold much faster.

Insulated ski pants, often simply called *snowpants,* are made very similiarly to parkas with a nylon shell and an insulation filling. There need not be as much filling as in a parka, and down, which is the most expensive insulating material is rarely necessary for children's ski pants. Some pants are filled with polyester and some with a lightweight non-bulky synthetic material known as Thermoslim. In selecting ski pants, look for many of the same quality features as in parkas — zippers, pockets, etc. These insulated ski pants are worn over long underwear.

I feel the best pants for children are the bib-overall styles. The bib part adds another layer of warmth and helps prevent the snow from getting up the back. As with the child's regular pant style, it is again important that the outside cuff goes over the boot and that there is an inside snow cuff. Elastic is essential around the waist and in the shoulder straps as it allows for greater movement. Some manufacturers insert "action panels" but these should be insulated. Watch closely that the snaps either on the waist or the bib straps work easily and that the pant legs are long enough.

"Warm-up" pants are made of thin nylon, sometimes with small amounts of insulation, and zip, or pull on, over jeans. They help break the wind, should be water-repellent, and can be an inexpensive alternative to stretch or snowpants. Check for quality of zippers and the nylon shell material.

Knickers are mostly used for ski touring but can easily be worn with long wool socks for Alpine skiing. They are mostly of corduroy and, unless they have been specially treated, they do get wet. In ski touring, you don't have cold chair lifts to ride so they are more suitable. Also ski knickers for children are hard to find.

Many manufacturers have coordinated parkas and pants. Some of these even zip together at the waist. Other suits are one piece and the parka cannot be worn separately, which is disadvantageous for older children. For small children, however, I do feel the one-piece suits are great to serve as all-purpose snowsuits as well as ski outfits.

A practical extra with certain ski pants is a "grow-seam" in the cuffs so they can be easily let out. Several styles can also be easily tucked up. Again, especially important in ski pants, as in any pant, are strong seams and a good fit with plenty of room for action.

Suggested Manufacturers:
  Alpenblick
  Aspen
  C.B. Sports
  Edelweiss
  Hot Gear
  JLB
  Obermeyer
  Profile
  Sears
  Skyr
  Sportscaster
  Swing West
Cost range: $12.00 - $14.00

VESTS

Ski vests are nonessential extras and can easily be omitted. However, they are marvelous for children and very comfortable. Vests are made exactly like parkas (minus the arms) so the same selection criteria would apply. They help keep the torso warm, and at the same time provide greater freedom of movement for the arms. They can be worn over a sweater, or over a sweater and windshirt, and because a vest is usually worn on a warm day, snaps instead of zippers are acceptable. Vests can be just as good for horseback riding, camping, bike riding, fishing, etc., so their use is not just restricted to skiing. They are extremely popular and surprisingly warm.

Suggested Manufacturers:
C.B. Sports
Hot Gear
Liberty Bell
Profile
Swing West
White Stag
Cost range: $18.00 - $38.00

HATS, HOODS, AND HELMETS

It is hard to believe how much body heat can escape from a bare head. This seems even more critical with children. My feeling is that hats should be worn at all times when skiing. There are so very few super-warm days that are exceptions, and even then the hat usually serves to protect the top of the ears from sunburn. Children are prone to ear infections, frostbite, and sunburn, and a good snug hat over the ears helps. Unfortunately, few manufacturers produce special children-sized hats and adult sizes may be too big. Many children, and adults, find acrylic less scratchy than wool on their foreheads. Perfectly adequate hats are probably already available at home. It need not have a pom-pom or snowflakes to be warm.

As mentioned, some parkas come with attached hoods. The non-insulated hoods, designed to go over a hat in a storm, are not adequate for headcover alone. The insulated hoods are great, yet can be almost too hot. If a child gets hot and sweaty and takes off his hood, get out the cold medicine.

Crash helmets, often referred to as "hard hats", are required in downhill races and many parents feel they offer necessary extra protection for fast, fearless young skiers. There is no question that they do protect a child's head. They should fit firmly but comfortably. Also, the child should be able to hear well with the helmet on which can be a problem as helmets do frequently muffle sound. If a small child is just beginning, or is skiing conservatively, he will not need a helmet. If, on the other hand, he is a very fast five- or six-year-old who jumps every bump and loves skiing between the trees, I'd definitely consider a helmet.

Suggested Manufacturers:
Hats
   Aris
   Hot Gear
   Kids Lids
   Mountain Lid
   Pussy Caps
   Wigwam
   Frostline Kits
Cost range: $5.00 - $12.00

Helmets
   Joffa
   Bell (Ski Imports)
   Scott
Cost range: $20.00 - $40.00

GLOVES AND MITTENS

Gloves and mittens should be well insulated and made from a tough, waterproof outer material such as leather, vinyl, or combinations of nylon and leather. This outer material has to be able to withstand quite a beating — ski edges, rope tows, binding hardwear, ice, snow and water. Gloves and mittens should never be too tight. They should come up well over, and fit snuggly around, the wrist. Most gloves have special knit or elasticized cuffs to keep them snug and prevent snow from getting inside. My preference for children is mittens because they seem much warmer and are definitely easier to take on and off. Some are even insulated with down which produces a marvelously warm mitten. Adequate waterproof gloves can be purchased even from the supermarket, yet keep in mind that the less insulation, and the thinner the outer shell, the colder the hands will be. There is no denying it; children's hands get cold very quickly.

Woolen children's mittens are not adequate. Snow cakes up on them, and they are not sufficiently warm or water-repellent. However, they can be worn as liners under another mitten. Special liners are also produced from silk and synthetics, including the latest aluminized space age material, and help provide a comfortable extra layer.

Suggested Manufacturers:
   Aris
   Conroy
   Kombi — including baby sizes
   Obermeyer
   Weiss
Cost range: $4.00 - $15.00

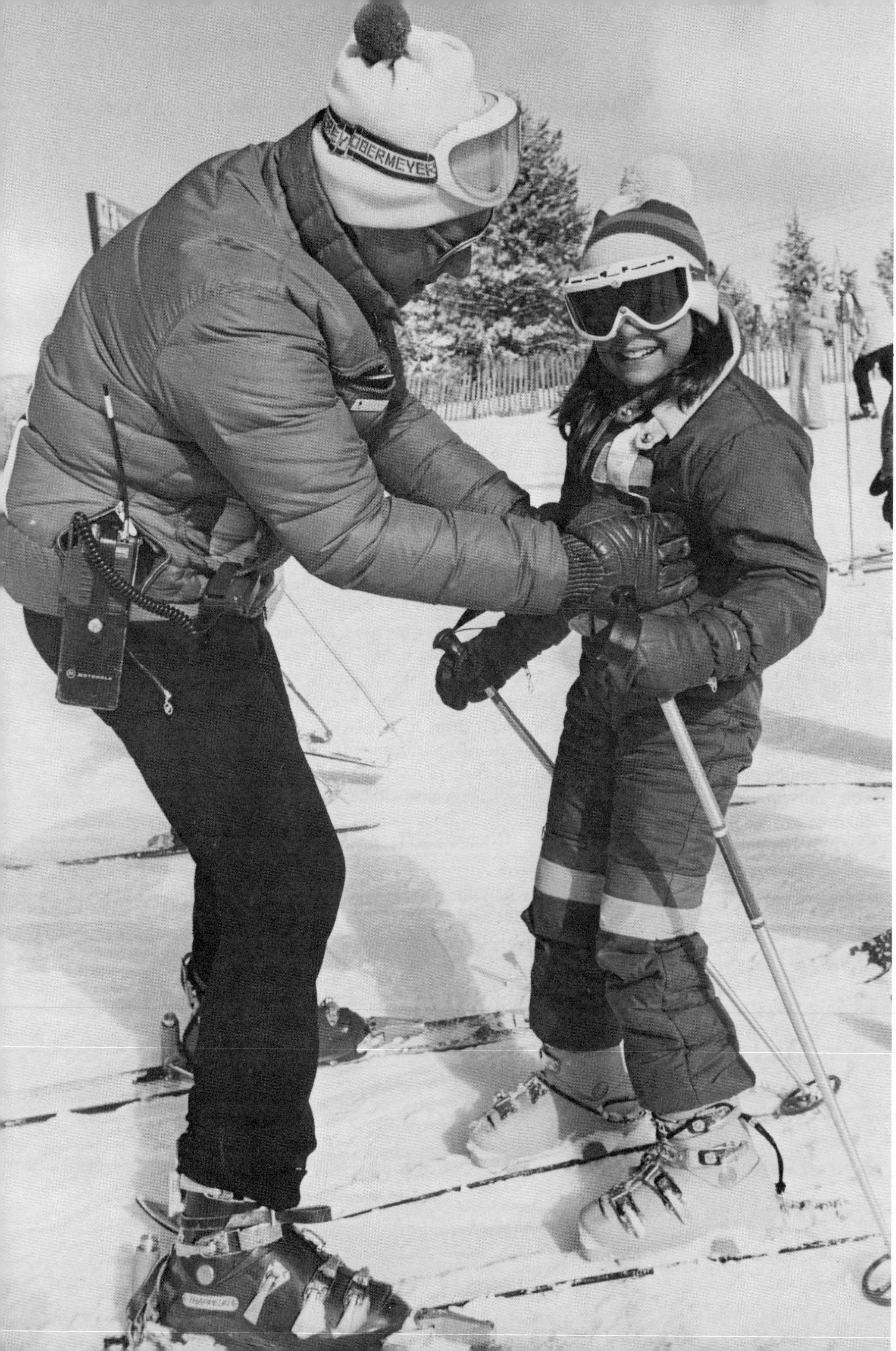

Vail photo by Peter Runyon

GOGGLES AND SUNGLASSES

Goggles and sunglasses, I feel, are as important as a parka or ski boots. They are essential, in fact, and more and more ski schools are requiring them. Children can, and have, become snow blind and have permanently damaged their eyes from skiing without them. There is also the problem of snow blowing into the eyes. My preference is to have a pair of children's size goggles with an all-purpose lens and to insist that the child wear them at all times. Be sure there is adequate padding around the frame so they fit comfortably. Models with changeable lenses, from a dark smoke color for sunny days, to yellow-amber for gray snowy days, are available, but switching lenses is usually too complicated for children so multi-purpose lenses seem more practical. Sunglasses, while available in small sizes, are more apt to fall off than goggles. Anti-fog cloths can be used to keep the lenses from fogging up. So, please, don't under any circumstances send your child skiing without goggles.

Suggested Manufactueres:
   Carrera
   Cebe
   Raichle Molitor
   Scott
   Uvex
Cost range: $4.00 - $12.00

ACCESSORIES OR EXTRAS

It is often hard to get past the bright display counters without adding extras and accessories. Some of these are already at home and unnecessary, and some, on the other hand, can be very useful and not just an added expense.

Ski Masks: These are knitted face and head covers with openings for eyes, nose, and mouth. Unfortunately, they are often associated with bank robberies, and small children can actually be frightened by them. Unless a ski mask really fits well, with all the openings at the right places, it is often more trouble than it is worth. If the day is that cold, the child probably shouldn't be skiing.

Scarves and Bandannas: These are often readily available at home. On a cold day a warm scarf is a welcome addition as it can be pulled up around the face on the lift and while skiing. Bandannas are stylish but do not provide the extra warmth a wool or acrylic scarf does. Avoid long wool scarves on small children unless the ends are tucked in. They could tangle in the lifts.

Suspenders: Special children's ski suspenders are available which clip on to knickers or ski pants, and can be helpful in holding up less-than-snug models.

Gaiters: There are two types of gaiters. The most common is worn over the top of the boot and fastens above the ankle to prevent snow from going down the boot. These are very necessary in ski touring and helpful in deep snow, especially if jeans are being used. I haven't found a child's gaiter, but the eight-inch size should be adequate. The other type, a neck gaiter, is of wool or acrylic for up-to-the-chin protection in swirling deep powder skiing and probably not necessary for children.

Fanny Packs: Fanny packs are small zipper bags on a belt and can be helpful for children to store their belongings. If they are not attached to the parka in any way, it is one more thing to be lost and most parkas do have ample pockets.

After-Ski Boots: A warm, comfortable, waterproof boot to change into immediately after skiing is great to have. If a child lives in a winter climate, he usually has such a boot and a special model is not necessary. Yet, after-ski boots can in turn be used as all-around winter boots as well. It is important that a child isn't expected to do lots and lots of walking in ski boots, which is awkward, uncomfortable and tiring for the child and not too good for the boots either.

> *Suggested Manufacturers:*
> Dunham
> Roces
> Tecnica
> *Cost range:* $12.00 - $35.00

TIPS ON PUTTING IT ALL TOGETHER

Now that I have listed all the varieties of clothing, parents may be discouraged by the quantity needed. Yet, some garments can be substituted and many are already in the wardrobe at home. The priority of items is as follows:

1. Goggles
2. Parka
3. Gloves/Mittens
4. Hat
5. Ski pants

If the child won't ski much during one season, jeans with gaiters and one or two pairs of long-johns (which can double as p.j.'s or vice versa) will be fine. Sweaters, hats, and turtle-necks the child probably already has.

There are lots of other tricks and ideas that can make skiing with kids so much easier, most of which have been discovered by trial and error.

1. Nametags should be on all children's clothing.

2. A piece of terrycloth attached to the glove or parka cuff with velcro or snaps, can do wonders for runny noses. The terry cloth can be detached and washed in the machine. In any case, the child should have plenty of tissue or handkerchiefs.

3. Clips and velcro patches serve to hook everything together. Gloves should be clipped to the parka cuffs. Hats should be clipped to the parka collar, and a small velcro dot sewn on the hat with the matching dot on the goggle head strap. This way when a child takes his parka off at lunch or whenever, everything is attached.

4. Identification cards should accompany children and be in a safe parka pocket, preferably an inside pocket. The following information should be included:

Child's name
Parents' name
Home address
Home phone
Local address and phone
Car license number
Car make and color

(If you drove, the car information is very useful, as cars are so often the meeting place.)

ALSO DON'T FORGET

Money for cocoa or a snack
Sunburn and lip cream
Tissue
A chocolate bar or raisins as an energy booster and morale builder

Herringbone or duck walk at Breckenridge; photo by Christi Northrop

III   Equipment

You've decided that your child is ready and willing to ski, and the necessary clothing is available from the cedar chest, the thrift shop, hand-me-downs, and nearby ski shops. It is now wise to think about acquiring ski equipment long before the snowflakes start to fall from the gray winter sky. For the best selection of new and used equipment, shop in October and early November to avoid the Christmas rush and harried clerks. Speaking of Christmas, Santa prefers to bring items that do not depend upon careful fit. He can bring hats, goggles, gloves, turtle-necks and vests. Santa can even bring unmounted skis if he has the child's height and knows his ability.

There are several ways to acquire the necessary ski equipment. You can either purchase new or used equipment, use hand-me-downs, or you can rent the equipment by the day, week, or sometimes season. All equipment must be in good skiable condition and checked out by a professional as poor or misfitting gear can not only cause injury but can completely discourage and frustrate a child. You wouldn't ask a child to ride a bike with a flat tire, and sending him out with poor equipment is not that much different.

The cost of fully equipping a child for skiing can be slightly astronomical, so shop carefully and don't overlook hand-me-downs. Many shops have family trade-in plans with fine used equipment or have new equipment that can be turned in next season for credit towards larger sizes. My preference is to deal with a shop that has such a "grow plan" to take advantage of the expertise of the shop personnel with the understanding that the used equipment has been examined and is safe. If used equipment is purchased at a ski-swap, thrift shop, or donated by a sibling or friend, it should definitely be taken to a reputable ski shop to be checked out. Most accidents occur on hand-me-down and used equipment which has not been tested. If you are lucky enough to have choices, try to find a shop that specializes in children's equipment. Try to deal with a salesman who is qualified and knowledgeable, and don't hesitate to ask for a second opinion. Above all, when shopping for equipment, new and used, allow plenty of time. It can be a lengthy process to properly fit boots and explain the bindings. Listen and don't rush.

Another alternative to purchasing equipment is to rent it. Ski equipment can be rented from a local ski or sports shop, or at the ski area you are visiting. However, it is essential that you check the availability of the necessary children's rental sizes before arriving at the area. Do investigate and compare costs, since some outlets rent children's equipment at much lower rates than others. Again, if you are renting, allow plenty of time to be fitted. At some shops or areas you can rent the evening before when it is far less crowded. If you are renting at the area, arrive early and allow for as long as an hour to get the equipment. Also take your driver's license and charge cards along for the required identification to take the equipment out. If you are only skiing a few times a season, renting is the answer. Try to figure roughly how many days the child will ski to compare the estimated rental costs with the cost of purchasing equipment and trading it in. A few places do rent by the season and this can be a great savings if the equipment is in good condition and the season rate is reasonable. Above all, when renting as well as buying, be sure the bindings are carefully fitted, the release checked and that you and your child understand *how* they work.

No equipment, free, purchased, or rented, is a good deal if any piece is not the proper size and length. Special children's ski packages are usually very reasonable, yet the quality, especially of the binding, is often sacrificed. Occasionally, a bargain ski package is worthwhile if the skis and poles are adequate. You can still exchange the binding for one that is safer and of better quality.

I feel it is always best to start at the ski shop, ask for professional advice and then, perhaps, shop around. Information from the ski shop can usually save dollars, time, aggravation, and in the long run can help avoid injuries.

Equipment can frequently be purchased to last more than one season. However, it is important not to allow for so much grow room that the child is unable to manage the first season. If a child is frustrated by skis that are too long and boots that require six pairs of socks, there may never be a second season. Allow for grow room if possible but don't sacrifice the fit.

BOOTS

Boots must support the ankle and foot, allowing the skier to edge, slide and turn properly on his skis. They are often considered the most important part of the equipment, and they definitely require time and patience from the child, parent, and salesman to be fitted well — the experience of fitting ski boots should be similar to fitting a one-year-old for his first walking shoes.

There are, basically, three types of boots: high plastic boots with an inner foam or synthetic bladder; small, low, rubber or vinyl kiddie boots; or old style leather lace or buckle boots. The main reason plastic has replaced leather is that it does not break down and soften as quickly or warp. Also, it offers excellent, lightweight support. If old style leather lace-up or buckle boots are available in good condition and do fit the child, they are perfectly acceptable, provided they are compatible with the binding. The low vinyl or synthetic boots usually come only in small sizes and are for pre-school nursery use. For the small three- or four-year-olds whose ski time is limited and playtime is great, these lower boots which come up to just above the ankle are perfectly adequate. If the child is older, riding lifts and turning a lot, he needs more ankle support and a stiffer, taller boot. I agree that the tall yellow or bright colored plastic boots look miserably uncomfortable and out of place on little feet, but actually they are surprisingly light and comfy. Because they don't cut into the front of the ankle as some lower boots do, many children like them far better.

Before going into further criteria for selecting and fitting ski boots, I should elaborate on boot-binding compatibility which can be so critical. If the sole is warped, too wide or too thick, it may not fit certain bindings. Most of the new boots now have soles that are nearly standard to fit bindings well at the toe and heel and slide with the anti-friction devices. This makes selecting the boot and binding much easier and allows for greater choice. With an older boot, a plate binding is usually the only compatible one so be prepared to hear about boot-binding compatibility and deal with it. If the boot doesn't come out of the binding when it is supposed to, something has to give and often it is a bone.

A child should try a boot on with the socks he plans to use. A quick way to tell if the boot is going to fit is to hold the bottom of the child's foot up against the sole of the boot. Most children's ski boots are made in Italy and, although they are supposedly in standard American sizes, the fit is a little different. New boots are stiff and good boots remain somewhat stiff so it takes patience to get into them. In selecting a boot, carefully check the following list of criteria:

1. The child should have plenty of toe room and be able to wiggle his toes. If he is curling his toes, gently press on the top of the boot so he will straighten them out.

2. When the child's foot is forward in the boot, you should be able to get at least one, preferably two fingers behind the heel.

3. When the heel is back in the proper position, it should not easily lift or slide around within the boot.

4. Be sure the child walks in the boots for ten to fifteen minutes to further assure that he is comfortable with the fit. Be watchful that a child is not simply complaining because he doesn't like the color, or brand, or because it's not the same sort the racers use.

5. He should be able to lean forward with his knees bent in a skiing position and not experience uncomfortable pressure points. Have him try this several times.

6. Plastic boots, contrary to popular belief, can be mechanically stretched and modified for a better fit if necessary.

7. Check that the buckles are well made, adjustable, and relatively easy to fasten and unfasten.

When shopping for a new boot, don't be brand conscious; fit is foremost, and style,

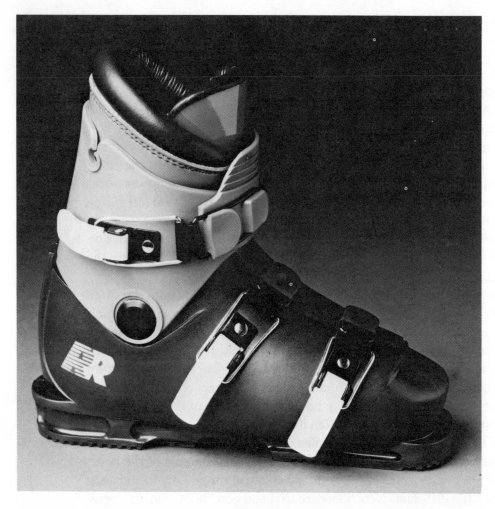

High boots with a Thermoplast shell and all-foam nylon inner boot; photo courtesy of Raichle Molitor U.S.A.

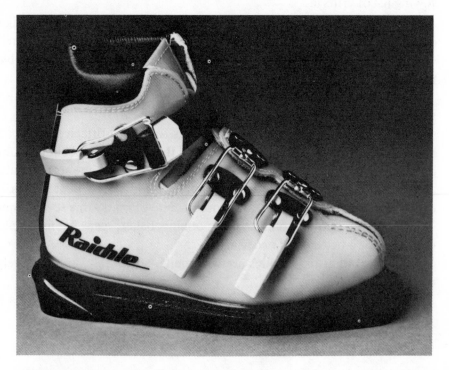

Small, low kiddie boots of plastic laminate; photo courtesy of Raichle Molitor U.S.A.

color, and brand are secondary. The construction of most junior boots is practically identical, so brand names are insignificant unless a guarantee is involved. And guarantees do not play a vital role with boots. Also be reminded that the Italian boots tend to be narrower than American lasts so be sure the feet are not cramped.

Suggested Manufacturers:
Low pre-school boots:
    A&T Comet
    Reicher (used)
    Raichle — Valbella Jr.
Cost range: $23.00 - $32.00

Regular junior boots:
    Alpina - Junior
    Caber - Star Junior 10 - 5
    Dynafit - Junior Cup 10 - 7
    Hanson - Simba
    Henke - Aprica Junior 12 - 6
    Koflach - Junior 12 - 5
    Nordica - Junior 9 - 9
    Raichle - Alpina Junior 12 - 6
            - Pacer Junior 1 - 6
    Roces - Baby 10 - 2
    San Marco - Junior 11 - 7
    Tecnica - Tiger 11 - 7
Cost range: $35.00 - $60.00

SKIS

Basically, children's skis should be very durable and have plenty of "flex". Flex is used to describe stiffness or lack of stiffness in a ski. A child's ski should be soft with lots of flex and able to absorb impact. Try bending various models to see the relative difference. Children learn quickly and before long they are jumping moguls and landing stiff legged on the flats where the ski must absorb the impact. Young skiers tend to be pretty hard on their skis, so the ski should be tough. When purchasing them, check to see if the manufacturer offers a one-year guarantee or has a low-cost replacement plan.

Most new skis are made with several layers of different materials such as wood, plastic, metal, and fiberglass. Try to examine a sample cut of the ski or ask for a brochure explaining the materials used. In buying a new or used ski, parents should look for the following:

1. *Flex:* A soft ski is far preferable to a stiff, racing model.

2. *Edges:* Inlaid hidden edges are more expensive but more durable and satisfactory. If screw-on edges are used, the sections should be flush, should fit together tightly and be well secured. Most toddler, or pre-school, skis come without edges.

3. *Length or size:* This depends a lot on the child's skiing ability and his general physical coordination and strength. Don't get skis that are too long. There are different schools of thought on ski length but a good general rule is:

Three- and four-year-olds — skis to the waist or lower chest.

Five- and six-year-olds — skis to the shoulder. Agressive six-year-olds and up — skis at eye level.

4. *Bottoms:* Bottoms should be as smooth as possible. Most new skis come with one of various synthetic plastic coatings. If the used ski bottom is badly gouged, it can be refinished, provided the rest of the ski is in good shape.

5. *Top finish and decoration:* The more durable the finish is, the better the ski will look and hold up after a season or two. Soft plastic finishes chip and gouge easily. Again, children are rough on skis and surface scratches are to be expected. Also, skis should not be purchased for their color, or stripes and brand logo.

6. *Warping:* It is important that used skis are not warped and that they are still flexible.

7. *Rusted edges:* Many edges rust in damp climates but if the rest of the ski is in good condition, the rust can be removed with steel wool and edges sharpened.

If economy is an issue, I would advise buying a less expensive ski or a good used one and saving pennies for boots and bindings. Boots and binding selection is far more critical for a child than ski selection. There are several perfectly adequate moderately priced skis, yet few adequate inexpensive bindings.

For toddlers and pre-schoolers who will ski only short periods of time, a short, light-weight, easy-to-manage ski is needed. The ski packages (skis, bindings, and poles) are recommended for this age group, but this age group only. Many of these skis are ABS molded

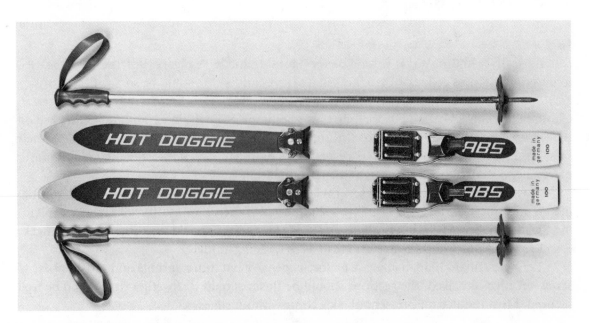

Pre-school skis of ABS molded plastic; photo courtesy of sarner fullplast america

Fishscale bottoms on pre-school skis make uphill climbing easier; photo courtesy of Trak, Incorporated

plastic. The construction and quality of plastic is being improved as some plastic skis had a tendency to break in very cold weather. These skis are really limited to one or sometimes two seasons since, as the child progresses, he needs a stronger, more substantial ski. Several regular junior skis do come in the 100 cm size and can also be considered for the pre-school skier as well.

The issue of edges on "baby" skis is somewhat controversial. The International Ski Safety Standards advise against metal edges on "baby", or pre-school, skis. Many ski instructors, however, prefer wooden construction with edges as opposed to lightweight solid plastic. I feel that small children usually have gloves on and are not often bothered by the edges. So, if you have a pair of small wooden skis in good enough condition, don't discard it because of the edges. Just advise the child to be careful.

Another important innovation in the design of toddler skis is the addition of "fishscale" bottoms. These bottoms are usually found on cross-country skis yet have now been introduced on small downhill skis for children. With this feature the child can climb uphill more easily, avoiding much frustration. The fishscales can be sanded off later if the child's progress warrants it. Pre-school skis are usually 70 - 100 cm. in length.

My preference is Trak Kidski with the fishscale bottoms. The following, all quite equal in quality, are listed alphabetically:

A & T - Blitz or Comet
Elan - Kid
Sarner - Hot Doggie
Cost range for pre-school skis: $20.00 - $30.00

Junior skis of fiberglass reinforced polyurethane, and high plastic boot; photo courtesy of Fischer of America, Inc.

Regular junior skis vary greatly in price according to materials used. As with ski boots many of the popular skis are made in the same factory and marketed under different brands. Parents should pay more attention to the guarantee, construction, durability, and price, than brand. Ski brands are like cereal brands; constantly changing with new names and new claims. I have selected a few of the better children's skis but excluded racing models and super high-cost models.

Suggested Manufacturers: (alphabetically)
A&T Fakon Jr., 90 - 160 cm.
Avanti Jr., 90 - 160 cm.
Champion Jr., 90 - 160 cm.
Hummer, 130 - 160 cm.
Elan Flex (red or blue), 100 - 170 cm.
Kids Impuls, 100 - 140 cm.
Erbacher - TC 77, 100 - 130 cm.
Fisher Jolly, 70 - 110 cm.
Blaze, 120 - 170 cm.
Hart Gremlin, 80 - 170 cm.
Head Junior, 110 - 150 cm.
Kastle Racer Jr., 100 - 140 cm.
Rossignol Smash, 100 - 140 cm.
Sarner Hop, 100 - 160 cm.
Volkl Tiger, 100 - 170 cm.
Cost range: $25.00 - $75.00

BINDINGS

The best advice I can give parents in this field is: *please don't scrimp.* Buy a new or used quality binding rather than a cheap "children's special". The binding not only holds the boot on the ski securely for maneuverability, but in the case of a fall or when excessive pressure is exerted on the binding, it releases the boot efficiently. It should release for both forward and lateral falls. Since children are capable of falling in odd ways and at strange angles the bindings must release under many different conditions.

Bindings (and the skis) are further attached to the boot by safety or "run-away" straps. These merely fasten on to the boot or around the boot so the ski will not slide off down the slope if the foot is released in a fall. If these straps are too long, the ski is apt to fly around or "windmill" and hit the child. Since younger children can easily get tangled up with safety straps, the simpler and more secure they are, the better. In attempts to avoid the possibility of windmilling, manufacturers have invented ski-brakes to replace straps. As the boot is released, a prong jabs down into the snow and holds the ski. I do not advise these for young children. In deep snow it is easy to lose the ski and have to prod and search with poles to find it. Also, children's bindings are usually set very loosely and can come off even on a lift — bye bye ski if it is equipped just with a ski-brake.

We hear the term AFD a lot in relation to bindings. The AFD is an "anti-friction device" placed on the ski directly behind the toe piece. Its purpose is to aid in the lateral release of the boot from the binding by eliminating friction between the boot, binding, and ski. AFDs, sliding pads of rubber, Teflon, or other synthetic materials, are an essential addition to assure a smooth working binding. Most new boots have soles constructed in such a way that a section of the sole surface fits directly on the AFD. AFD is not a secret code. It is important for a good release system.

There are basically three main types of bindings:

1. *Cable bindings* — Twenty years ago this was "the" binding. The cable actually goes around the heel and is secured in front of the toe with a latch or lever device. The toe piece does allow for lateral release but the binding rarely allows for forward release. These are best used on small pre-school skis and many come pre-mounted. A similar version of the cable binding is very popular on children's touring sets. For an older child's alpine binding, however, I do not recommend cable bindings.

2. *Step-in bindings* — The child literally steps into the binding and closes it by stepping down. These are very convenient and most adequate as they release with both lateral and forward pressure. The heel-piece releases well especially in those head-forward, somersault falls kids are noted for. While step-in bindings are fairly simple to operate, the child should avoid fiddling with the binding. The spring loaded heel-piece is like a mousetrap and could be extremely dangerous if a small finger were caught in it.

3. *Plate bindings* — A plate attaches to the boot and then to the heel and toe pieces on the ski. These bindings are extremely safe with excellent release and are good because they can accommodate a wider variety of boot soles. Also in this grouping is a simple but excellent style that has a heel spring and heel plate only, no toe piece, but used with an AFD. The plate bindings may look like a lot of hardwear and very complicated but they are actually quite simple, easy for children to use, and very safe.

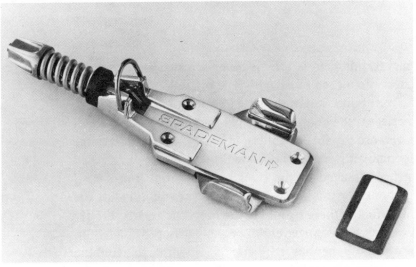

ABOVE: Plate binding for juniors; photo courtesy of Spademan Release Systems

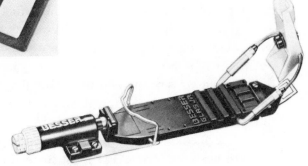

ABOVE: Glas Jr. plate binding; photo courtesy of Besser

BELOW: Binding with front and rear lateral and vertical releases; photo courtesy of Americana International

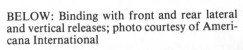

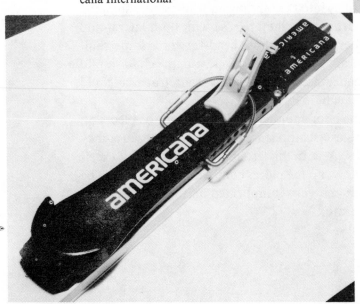

ABOVE: Step-in 101 binding for children; photo courtesy of Salomon/North America

With any binding, be sure you *fully* understand how it works and ask for a brochure to help remind you. When selecting bindings, parents should definitely be brand conscious as bindings are not of similar quality. Many manufacturers sponsor special workshops, so the shop personnel are further certified to sell, adjust, and service the particular binding. Also major manufacturers will stand behind their brands. Brands are important.

Manufacturers set a certain weight specification for their bindings such as 45 - 100 lbs. It is very important to be sure your child is within the given weight range. Otherwise, it cannot be assured that the binding will release.

It is especially important to realize that bindings can be taken off and remounted from ski to ski. With the exception of the toddler pre-school bindings, parents can usually buy a binding for a five- or six-year-old which will last until he is about twelve or weighs 100 lbs. Generally he can then move into an adult binding that is set for the lighter weight. Binding expense need not be a yearly ordeal, which is a relief.

Again, do not try to adjust the bindings on your own. Ski shops have very sophisticated machines by which they can accurately adjust the binding based on weight, leg bone size, and ability. It is a good idea to have parents' equipment re-checked for binding release as well. Unfortunately, several law suits have arisen over binding adjustment, so don't be astonished if a ski instructor sends your child to the ski repair shop for adjustments rather than handling it himself. Ski area personnel and shop personnel are very careful when handling bindings because of the legal ramifications. So, in summary, don't scrimp and do turn the binding matter over to the experts.

I have listed the binding manufacturers in order of my preference based on a season's research. I'm sure there are conflicting opinions but hopefully this will serve as a guide to you as parents.

Recommended Manufacturers:
Step-in
    Solomon 101 45 - 100 lbs.
    Solomon 111 50 - 120 lbs.
    Solomon 444 70 - 200 lbs.
    Tyrolia-50 Jr. 30 - 130 lbs.
    Allsop-Jr. 50 - 100 lbs.
    (Allsop has excellent safety straps as well)

Plate bindings:
    Besser - Child glas 25 - 75 lbs.
    Besser - Junior glas 50 - 140 lbs.
    Spademan - Junior 40 - 90 lbs.
    Americana Junior 50 - 100 lbs.
Cost range: $25.00 - $70.00

POLES

Poles are relatively inexpensive and can last a few seasons. Again parents need not be too brand conscious. Often, ski shops have special-sale poles which are perfectly adequate. The pole should be sturdy, preferably metal or a very strong plastic for the little guys. Children must respect pole tips as they can be dangerous since poles are seldom used properly by children when skiing. However, they are essential for walking, climbing and balancing.

To chose the correct height or length of pole for a child, have the child grip the pole upside down directly under the basket with the handle end touching the floor. If the child's arm is at a 90° angle to his body, the pole height is correct. Do not buy poles which are too long. The child is better off with a slightly shorter pole than one that is long and unwieldy.

Suggested Manufacturers:
  A&T
  Barrecrafter
  Krystal
  Scott
  Tomic
Cost range: $4.00 - $10.00

Ski equipment accessories are frequently very valuable, and often an inexpensive addition that will make ski trips so much more enjoyable.

Ski fasteners are essential, in my mind, to keep the skis together for carrying and storing. If you have ever watched a child struggle across a parking lot without ski fasteners, you will gladly purchase these clips or straps. Some ski shops even give them away. One type goes around the skis and poles, with the poles thus becoming a carrying handle. Ski fasteners come in combinations of rubber and metal, velcro, or plastic. They *are* needed and they are cheap.

Ski boot trees or carriers were required with leather boots to prevent warping. The new plastic boots don't warp much but it is a good idea to use them so the child can easily carry his boots and keep them together. Nothing is worse than getting home to find out your child has dropped a boot in the parking lot.

Wax can be necessary for certain snow conditions, especially on children's less expensive or worn ski bottoms. If a parent takes the time and waxes the child's skis, a potentially disastrous day of sticky snow can be turned into a wild success. If in doubt as to which color wax to use on what snow, check with the ski shop or instructor.

Silicone spray: When the shop salesman suggests the purchase of a silicone spray, you will probably shudder and think—not something else! Yet one can lasts a long time. One squirt and the binding's set for the whole day or two. The silicone protects the binding from ice, mud, rust and corrosion, and also aids in reducing friction between the binding and the boot which helps assure that the bindings will release and function smoothly.

Ski and boot bags are not at all necessary although an eleven-year-old could probably do a bang-up job convincing you he needs a $20.00 ski bag with the same imprinted brand name as on his skis or bindings. If you are traveling by air, most airlines provide free strong plastic ski bags. Also many junior skis fit in with parents skis in some of the larger ski bags.

Boots can be carried with a ski boot carrier or in a separate bag, and not necessarily a ski boot bag with matching logo.

Ski locks: Usually ski locks are more trouble than they are worth. There are several types yet they all involve either keys or combinations, and practically always the help of a parent or instructor.

In summary, start with boots, then skis and bindings and poles, but pay special attention to boots and bindings. One last thought is to clearly mark all equipment with names to identify its owner since many kids on the slope may have otherwise identical and easily confused gear. The problem of mistaken identity or theft is often a serious one. If skis and poles are left outdoors when a visit to the base lodge is necessary, either find some way to lock them up or (as we do) put one ski and pole in one rememberable spot and the matching pair in another. It is unlikely that anyone, by mistake or on purpose, will remove one ski and pole for any reason.

If you choose to leave the equipment together in one spot, be sure you remember where it is so that *you* are not guilty of walking off with the wrong gear. A special mark, such as a painted stripe or insignia, or better yet, your own name prominently and indelibly marked will insure unmistakeable recognition.

IV

Learning to Ski

Now that the equipment is purchased, borrowed, or rented for the season and is standing in the closet, it looks strange and foreign. Young children seem puzzled that their ski equipment isn't in the toy category. With the bright new colors of skis and the shiny bindings, the items look as if they belong in the playroom. A small child may keep asking about what this stuff is that I've tried on and why can't I use it as soon as I get home? There is good reason to introduce him to the mechanics before you reach the slopes. If, however, you've decided to rent equipment on a daily basis, try acquiring it the night before and then go over it with the child in your lodge.

With a little time, patience, and careful instruction, children can soon learn how to handle their equipment and, before long, how to master those silly boards which are attached to cumbersome stiff boots with lots of hardware. I cannot repeat too often that without patience on the parent's part, no child will ever learn to ski. It requires as much or more patience in dealing with equipment as it does actually skiing with kids. If all goes well, before you know it, your child will be gliding down mountain slopes with skis, body and snow in complete harmony.

To achieve the ultimate goal of mastering the sport, very careful attention must be given to the presentation of the equipment to the child. How a child is introduced to skiing is critical and the parent's role is so very important. Whether the parent decides to turn the whole matter over to the ski school and let them do the teaching or whether he tries to introduce the first stages at home, the parent must still prepare the child. By preparing him, I mean telling him what skiing is all about, explaining why he needs this or that piece of equipment and what he will be trying to do with it. If the child has seen older brothers or sisters or his parents ski, this explanation is very easy. If the child has never seen snow or skiing, it is good to show him some pictures, or, ideally, take him to a movie at your local ski club.

Once you have the feeling that the child has begun to understand what skiing is all about, you can begin introducing all the equipment. Personally, I feel if you have the gear at home you should definitely have the child become familiar with it prior to going to the ski area. So much can be learned at home. Boots can be worn around the house for short periods of time to accustom the child to the feel of the boot. The child probably has never had his foot in anything as stiff and confining. It will take a little time to become used to this sensation. If the boots are high, it is advisable to unbuckle the top buckles for walking until the child feels more comfortable. Also, encourage the child to learn to buckle and un-buckle his own boots. Wearing the boots around the house gives the parent the opportunity to be sure that the right number of socks or the right size sock is being worn.

Skis need not be kept in the closet until one reaches the ski area. Children and adults should try their skis on at home and be sure they understand exactly how the binding works. Getting used to bindings with a cold wind whipping around can be horrendous when it is easy to learn about them in a nice, cozy, warm home. Children should learn to handle as much of their own equipment as possible. If they can learn to put their bindings on and off and attach and detach the safety straps, the parents are several steps ahead. Bindings are a very important part of the ski equipment but appear somewhat complicated. Be sure, of course, you understand exactly how the binding works yourself. Many binding manufac-turers supply brochures describing the binding and you ought to read the instructions care-fully or go over the operation at the ski shop with an expert. Parents should avoid making adjustments on their own since most bindings are best adjusted according to a prescribed formula. Be sure, prior to leaving the rental or ski shop, that you, as parents, understand not only how the binding operates but that it has been properly adjusted to your child's boot. Even if your child is using hand-me-downs from his brother or sister, you must have these checked by an expert to be sure they will fit and release properly.

Once a child is comfortable in his boots and understands his bindings, he can actually become familiar with the skis and the feel of the skis. A lot of skiing can be learned at home. I refer to it as backyard skiing, though skis, even with metal edges, do little harm to carpets. A child can learn to slide and glide inside the house. I would suggest leaving the poles outside, however. The indoor carpet of the playroom is an ideal place for a young child to learn to walk on skis. It is not cold and a child is in very familiar surroundings. If a smooth, grassy bank is available, children can also practice walking outside but avoid too much maneuvering because one might hit a hidden rock and cause some damage. A child will be way ahead in the learning process if he can become familiar and relaxed with the feel of his skis.

For those lucky enough to live where it snows and with access to a yard or neighboring park, most of the basic beginning steps can be easily learned. Whether a child is learning to ski at the ski area or in his backyard, parents must take into consideration the weather, the terrain, (by terrain I mean if the hill is too steep, too bumpy, or too flat), and the general snow condition. A child can get just as cold in his own backyard as he can on a mountain. I personally find it is best to introduce skiing to young children in short time segments, perhaps only ten or fifteen minutes each day. If the child becomes frustrated, change to sledding, or build a snowman. Emphasize the fun of being in the snow. Older children can probably stand a half an hour or less of instruction. After a while, the child, old or young, will welcome a change or the introduction of a game, perhaps even with skis on.

Of equal importance to the parents' patience is the need for the child to have fun. Skiing should not be a torture, it should be recreation. Practically all parents, skiers and even non-skiers, can introduce ski equipment to their children, assist them in the process of becoming familiar with it and perhaps in learning to walk on the skis. However, from this point on, many parents prefer to turn the teaching directly over to professionals at ski schools. Other parents may choose to teach some more at home and help children learn the basic beginning phases of skiing.

If a child is familiar with his skis, boots, and poles and feels comfortable walking with them, he will probably progress more rapidly during the first ski school class and most likely be up the mountain sooner. To actually carry the early teaching further, a lot depends upon where the family lives and the parents' time and own skiing and teaching ability.

Before expanding on the different techniques and steps in teaching a child to ski, whether in a ski school or with a parent as teacher, all parents must carefully consider the following.

1. Be sure your child is feeling well and in good physical shape.
2. Be sure your child is adequately dressed and with goggles or glasses.
3. Be sure the equipment is in good shape with properly adjusted bindings, rust free ski edges, ice free ski and boot bottoms, and waxed ski bottoms if necessary.
4. Be sure your child knows what the story is — where he is to go, what he will be doing, etc.
5. Remember each child progresses at his own rate, so don't expect too much.
6. Has your child been to the bathroom?

Should parents teach their children to ski? This question is a common subject of debate with many pros and cons on both sides. While there seems to be little problem with the early introductory stage, teaching a child to ski beyond the basics, at the ski area, can be compared to teaching a wife to drive. A few parents can instruct their children magnificently and completely. When a parent is undertaking the complete instructional responsibility, he must be prepared to devote himself fully to this purpose and be willing to sacrifice his own skiing time. Teaching a child to ski beyond the early stages involves a lot more than showing a child how to ride a bicycle and alas, there are only a very few parents who have the combination of patience, good teaching skills and good skiing ability. I certainly admire these parents. My preference and suggestion is to teach the child the early stages at home and then to enroll the child in a ski school.

On the other hand, some parents feel very strongly that skiing is a family sport and all members should ski together. I feel a child can learn much from watching his brothers and sisters and he can benefit from his attempts to copy them. Yet, there should only be one instructor in the family and this should be decided upon prior to reaching the ski area. The one ski instructor, father or mother, or competent older brother or sister, should be totally responsible for teaching the beginner child and not be aided or contradicted by other family members. Children learning with their families should never feel under pressure to reach the level of ability of the older brothers and sisters overnight. Ideally, they should feel relaxed at all times and simply have an active, happy day. Such families are few and far between and I still feel the beginner best benefits from ski school lessons where he is among peers at his own ability level. When he has gained confidence and mastered his turns, he can then join the family, but still with only one family instructor.

As mentioned before, many parents, depending upon geographic location, can participate in teaching their children the first stages of skiing in advance near home. The main objective in this situation is for the child to become familiar with his equipment. The child can start to get the feel of really skiing. The following can serve as a guide to backyard skiing.

1. *Introduce the child to ski terms* and teach him the names of the parts of his skis: ski tip, ski tail, inside and outside edge, pole basket, pole strap.

2. *Walking on skis:* This is surprisingly easy and natural for children. Have them simply follow you and be sure the ground is level. Quickly they will learn to slide one ski at a time. This can be learned with or without poles.

3. *Falling and getting up:* For adults this can be a difficult maneuver but for children it poses little trouble as they are used to falling and getting up. Most children find their own best way to get up. Young children, however, can often have more difficulty, and it is better to offer them a hand than to make them struggle and tire themselves out. Encourage a child to sit down if he feels he is going to fall. He should be told not to fall forward or put out his arms to stop himself. He should be taught to relax and fall. One key to getting up, especially for older children, is to have them move their skis together, aligned across the hill. Then, with the body crouched close to the boot, the child pulls himself up on his two ski poles which are held perpendicular to his skis. The baskets and tips are planted in the snow on the uphill side, giving the child the necessary leverage.

4. *Ski poles:* My feeling is that ski poles are definitely a part of skiing and a child should get used to handling them and skiing with them at a very young age. Certain exercises are well learned without poles, yet if they are introduced in early stages, children will easily learn to use them. Children should be reminded how dangerous ski poles can be and warned not to wave them about or point them at other people.

5. *Bar exercises:* If you happen to have a swing set in your backyard with a cross bar on it or even a fence rail or low tree limb, this serves as a marvelous teaching aid. The child can lean on or hold the bar and balance himself. Holding onto the bar, he can learn to step from side to side with his skis, to slide one ski forward, one ski back, and also hop on skis. By holding onto the bar with two hands, again for extra balance, the child can even learn to sink down and push his skis out in a "V" to form a snowplow or 'piece of pie'. He also can learn the feeling of bending his knees and leaning forward. Such exercises are marvelous for

young children as they help make them feel secure on their skis which will help avoid many unnecessary falls.

6. *Side-stepping:* If you are fortunate enough to have a gentle hill nearby or even in the backyard, you can introduce the process of side-stepping up a hill. If not, the child can still learn the feeling of stepping from one ski to another and walking sideways across a flat surface. This can also be practiced on the bar. Actually, side-stepping up a hill can be somewhat difficult for small children, so if they get discouraged, do not force the issue. The child must bend his knees, use his edges, and, at the same time, lift one ski and then the other, which can be very confusing and frustrating. One idea that often works is to have a child take off his skis and climb the hill sideways using the edge of the sole of his boot as he would skis. Have him also climb a set of stairs sideways. Remember, the skis must always be across the hill and the knees bent forward slightly into the hill. It is not a bad idea to make some sort of game out of side-stepping with a reward waiting at the top of the hill.

7. *Help for getting up the hill:* Don't insist that small children climb up for their first run down. It is important that they get the feel of skiing before getting discouraged by such maneuvers as side-stepping. Small children can easily be carried up a short hill or they can hold on to their poles with the straps while you pull them up. It is best that you hold the tip end to prevent any danger or scratches. Another way to help the child up the hill is to have him bend his knees slightly while you push from behind, which will somewhat simulate riding a ski tow.

8. *Herringbone or duck walk:* This alternate method for climbing is sometimes so natural for children that they need no instruction. The skis are pointed uphill with tips apart and the tail ends together forming a "V". Poles are implanted behind and beside the body for support and to keep the child from slipping backward. The inside edges are biting into the hill holding the skis from slipping too. This looks like a duck walk and small children might enjoy a bit of quacking as they go up.

9. *Straight run:* The proper body position for the straight run or descent of the hill can be practiced while at the bar. Skis are together, knees and ankles bent forward. The straight run is best introduced without poles; the child placing his hands on his knees. Remind the child to look up and ahead towards where he is going. Since this is a somewhat ape-like position, and children love to imitate monkeys, a bit of silliness is not out of place and it relaxes them. Yet, above all, be sure there is a good outrun at the bottom of the hill so that stopping is not a problem and the child does not become frightened by an upcoming tree or fence. Descending the hill in the straight run position is the best way to introduce the child to what skiing really feels like. It can be repeated again and again as a child usually has a lot of fun doing it. Even if the parent has to help the child up the hill, I encourage the parent to endure and repeat this several times so the child comes to enjoy it and gets some real confidence in descending the hill in a straight run position.

10. *Snowplow or wedge:* The snowplow or wedge is somewhat complicated and difficult to learn. Most parents prefer to turn this phase of skiing over to the ski school as they are equipped with many inventive tricks and are experienced in teaching lots of children how to form a wedge and how to stop themselves with a wedge or snowplow stop. If the

parent attempts to teach the child this technique at home in the backyard, he should remember that the phase may require more patience than any other. Do not force the child if he becomes discouraged. A wedge requires a good deal of muscle control and strength and for some very young children who lack the necessary muscular development it can be very difficult. The wedge or snowplow can best be demonstrated by using the bar to assist in balance. As the child sinks down with his knees and ankles bent forward, he pushes his heels or the tails of his skis out and forms a V. Remember, when using the term V, that many young children do not yet know their alphabet. Describe it as a piece of pie which most will recognize. They can best learn by watching it demonstrated. As the child pulls his skis together, he rises up again. This can be repeated many times at the bar and the child will begin to get a good sense of pushing the tails of his skis out. Young children can sometimes learn the proper wedge position and the feel of the wedge or snowplow by descending the small hill between the parent's legs. This is a teaching exercise, and it should be noted that it is not a good habit to get into. It can be somewhat dangerous, and the child can become too dependent upon the parent or instructor.

Another teaching aid is for the parent to position himself just downhill from the child to help keep the ski tips close together. By having the tips steady, the child can concentrate on pushing the tails of his skis out. Learning a snowplow or wedge stop from a straight run position can be even more discouraging. Yet, this is a place where games can easily be introduced. If the child is playing a game, he forgets the strenuous learning, becomes relaxed and therefore performs better. If the child has trouble with his ski tips continually crossing, try to encourage him to let the ski tips just "kiss" each other but not "hug" each other. To stop with a snowplow or wedge, the child must definitely sink down and be able to push the tails out properly.

In my opinion, these ten maneuvers and the parents' own variations on them are the full extent of what should be taught in backyard sessions. From this point on, a child needs a good slope for teaching terrain and good snow conditions too. If parents continue to teach their children at the area, they must be sure to cover the following phases.

1. Wedge turns
2. Traverse positions
3. Sideslipping
4. Beginning parallel stops, often referred to as racing or hockey stops. From there, the parent works into the stem turns.
5. Christies
6. Parallel turns

I will not try to cover these teaching steps in detail as I feel they are best handled in ski school with other children and trained instructors. Again, I repeat that parents who can teach children, from beginning stages to the more advanced, are unfortunately rare. Yet, as even those parents reach the more advanced stages, they should be sure to teach only the technique or style which they themselves employ. I have often heard some who are teaching their friends say, well, I can't really show you how to do it, but it should be done thus-and-so. In teaching children, this won't work. Children need a clear demonstration as to exactly

Learning to side-step; photo courtesy of Sun Valley

how the maneuver is performed and how it looks. Therefore, the parent-teacher should be proficient in the style or technique and able to demonstrate all levels of it.

SKI SCHOOLS

What are they all about and what is involved? If possible, children should be placed in the ski school after they have finished the backyard sessions at home or at least after they have become acquainted with their equipment. In some cases parents have neither the choice of teaching the child at home nor the opportunity of familiarizing him with the equipment because they are renting it at the ski area. In this case, the ski school should be able to fulfill these assignments, especially if the child has been verbally prepared by parents. Kids seem to learn as much from their peers as from instructors and parents, and thus, group classes, provided they aren't too large, seem to me to be the best answer to learning to ski. Even if a child skis a few times a year, group lessons are well worth-while, and from the experience he will come to enjoy the sport much more.

What makes a children's ski school good? It is very important to enroll your child in a school that has classes for children only, even if this means going to a ski area that does not offer the most exciting terrain for the parents. Unfortunately, perfect children's set-ups at a ski area are few and far between. Yet, it is wise to look for as many of these attributes as possible when selecting a particular children's ski school and ski area.

1. The ski area facilities should be centralized and not extremely spread out. The child should be able to find his way about without much difficulty.

2. Ideally two ski school programs are offered—one for the pre-schoolers from two and one half to five years, and another for the school-age children five to six years through twelve to fourteen.

3. Pre-school ski school should ideally be run in connection with the nursery so the little guys can easily retreat for naps, games, and lunch. Pre-school lessons should be shorter, about an hour in the morning and another hour in the afternoon, if the child is interested. The emphasis should absolutely be on play and fun with an introduction to the beginning skills and fundamentals. I feel strongly that there should be no more than five children per instructor for the pre-school classes.

Most of the following criteria for school-age children's ski schools can easily apply to pre-schoolers as well, with certain adjustments.

4. Children's instructors are so very obviously important. They should not only be specially trained to teach children, but, above all, they must really love young people and be able to spend their day happily with them. A genuine love and interest in children should take priority over excellent skiing ability. These instructors should understand children at various age levels and be able to communicate easily on that level. Perhaps children's instructors need even more patience than parents. They must not only teach skiing but be able, as relative strangers, to inspire a relaxed and trusting relationship—no easy task. Both parents and instructors must always remember that skiing is a very strange and foreign experience for many children.

It is also very important that children's instructors are responsibly mature and well organized. They should be well informed concerning terrain, weather, snow conditions, and the varied physical abilities of the class. Good instructors are worth their weight in gold and often don't receive the credit they deserve.

5. The teaching area should be separate and roped off to both protect the children from other skiers and to let them feel that this is their own turf. The teaching area should be on a gentle slope with a good outrun, and not too far from the meeting area. A long walk becomes both discouraging and tiresome. In addition, it should be conveniently located close to the warming house or nursery for cocoa breaks or bathroom visits. There should be enough room so that the children do not feel restricted, yet not so large that they feel lost within the area. The ski area should pay careful attention that the snow condition has been well maintained within this children's area as a good surface is essential for good instruction.

6. A terrain garden or ski playground is an area for children only, as it is designed to the scale of children's length skis. It may consist of obstacle courses and man-made bump formations such as a series known as the roller coaster or another called bicycle bumps. As kids go through these courses, sometimes using balls, balloons or other toys, they become so intent on the play aspects of what they are doing that they forget about trying to ski and their knees and skis respond and react naturally. They have fun and before you know it, they are acquiring some advanced ski skills such as separate weighting and edge control. In my opinion, a ski area that has been willing to spend the time, effort, and cost to create and maintain such a terrain garden deserves special praise.

7. A special children's lift is another ideal extra at children's areas. The lift is often connected with the terrain garden or ski playground, but it is specially constructed for children and assists them in getting up to the obstacle courses, enabling them to take several runs. The nature of these lifts can vary greatly from special pony lifts (similar to rope tows but with handles) to poma lifts. The height and speed should be adjusted for children.

If the particular area you are considering offers a ski school that provides all seven of these services, you and your kids are lucky and should have few problems. I admit that I have described an ideal facility but such do exist.

I wish to briefly mention the problems of children on ski lifts. Much depends upon the type of lift and the parent's own familiarity with it. If the child has been in ski school to any extent, he most likely will have been taught exactly how to prepare to load. Do go over it again. Before approaching the lift, the parent and child should decide on which side of the lift the child will ride; preferably the lift attendant's side as he then may assist the child. The parent and child should also discuss where to look, which hand will hold the poles, and which hand will be free. If the child is well prepared, many accidents that occur when loading and unloading a lift can be avoided. Parents should take notice of whether the lift operator is slowing the lift down for small kids to load. If not, the parent should kindly insist that this be done. A disastrous loading experience can scare a child terribly and turn him off skiing for a long time. These mishaps can be so easily avoided with the help of alert lift operators. Gondolas and trams usually pose less problems since they are loaded while standing still. Yet, children will often need assistance in removing their skis from the racks.

If a child is afraid of a T-bar or poma lift, he should merely watch others loading and riding for a while. The parent, without wearing his own skis, can simulate a poma lift experience by placing a ski pole between the child's legs and gently pulling him up the slope. T-bar practice can be accomplished by facing the child, holding the ski pole under his seat, and walking backwards uphill, thereby pulling him up. Always insist that the child keep his skis straight up the hill with knees bent, and that he leans on the bar but does not sit down.

Before riding all lifts, especially rope tows, it is necessary to check for loose equipment or clothing which could become tangled or caught in the lift.

Before even considering going up any lift, however, the child should be proficient enough in skiing back down; able to come to a complete stop in the fall line and able to turn well in both directions.

Ski etiquette is important, not only for good manners but safety too, and both parents and instructors should impress upon children the value of being polite and courteous on the slopes and in the lift lines. It is not uncommon to hear skiers proclaim: "Some little kid nearly ran me over." If ski etiquette were properly emphasized this frequent exclamation from a hassled skier would seldom be heard. Parents should insist that children wait their turn in lift lines and never cut in. Also while on the slopes children should watch for skiers in front of them. If they feel they absolutely must pass they should call "track right" or "track left", assuming the child knows right from left, or "passing on the inside or outside" if not. Personally, I don't think children should be encouraged to pass or call track until they are reasonably advanced.

Unfortunately, as the sport has grown in popularity, courtesy seems to have greatly declined. Hopefully parents and instructors can help bring forth a new generation of thoughtful, courteous skiers.

Again I stress that whether you enroll your child in a well qualified ski school or teach him to ski yourself, remember that skiing is a sport to be enjoyed and should be fun. Don't push for progress, push for enjoyment.

Riding the poma lift; photo courtesy of Keystone International

V
Ski Touring

Ski touring is definitely for the whole family. It might be wise to clear up the confusion between "ski touring" and "cross-country" skiing. While cross-country is mostly used in reference to racing and ski touring describes the recreational side of the sport, the terms are interchangeable. There are also many misconceptions about ski touring, the most obvious of which is that it is very strenuous. We are used to seeing pictures of great cross-country racers huffing and puffing to the finish line after a grueling 30 or 50 kilometer race. One does not think of a sunny afternoon on a golf course with grandmothers and young children all out for a short tour. For generations the Scandanavians have participated in ski touring as a family sport. Only recently have Americans begun to discover it and as a result, it is one of the fastest growing sports in the country.

Ski touring advocates are not faced with massive parking lots, expensive lift tickets, crowded cafeterias, and long lift lines. Instead they are silently gliding through snow-filled woods with a picnic lunch in a knapsack. Parents will be surprised to see how well their children can manage on cross-country skis. Ski touring should be a low keyed and relaxed activity, and it is my hope that the sport will remain this way. As the sport grows, however, strong elements of commercialization creep in. More expensive ski equipment, exotic and costly fashions, and higher trail fees are the result. Whether a family takes its cross-country equipment out to the local golf course, a city park, or actually goes to a touring center, a relaxed atmosphere is best for all concerned. No member of the family should ever feel pushed or competitive in keeping up with the others. If a family is already on a ski vacation,

The author's son ski touring near Winter Park; photo by Ned Northrop

an afternoon of touring offers a pleasant and welcome change of pace. Children, even as young as four, will be able to master the gear. Yet, the child will succeed best if the parent supports him and shows that he feels that the child can do it. If the parent says, "Well, we'll try, but I don't think Johnny will make it," it is nearly guaranteed that Johnny won't make it. If, on the other hand, the parent says, "Johnny and I will come along at our own pace, and meet you soon," then Johnny will be better able to manage. Children also do not respond as well to nagging as they do to a pep-talk. Walking on skis is fairly natural for children and once walking and sliding on skis is demonstrated to a child, he will rapidly pick it up. Before long, he will be gliding effortlessly along the trails with his parents. Also, as less technique is involved in the early stages of ski touring, detailed lessons are not really as important for children. Parents can familiarize the child with the equipment in much the same way as with Alpine equipment and once a child is familiar with either Alpine or Nordic, he can more easily adapt to the other.

When parents are considering a ski tour with children, it is essential that they plan carefully before departing. While it is always wise to check the weather before setting out, it is especially important when children are included. To be caught in a miserable storm will obviously damage the prospects of any future trips. The length and the terrain of the tour should also be carefully examined, with the age and ability of each child taken into consideration. Also, the parent ought to know the course and exactly where he is going. Being lost in the winter woods could prove to be a frightening experience for a child and perhaps a parent too.

Double check that children are adequately dressed with plenty of warm clothing, in layers which they can add or take off as the weather changes or they warm up from the exercise. Knapsacks should be filled with extra snacks and drinks as children become thirsty and hungry more rapidly than adults, and a quick snack or piece of candy can help make the trip much more enjoyable. First aid supplies should not be forgotten since no ski-patrol is likely and it may be a long way back or to the nearest farm or phone. Again, depending upon the ages and abilities of the children, plenty of rest stops should be taken so no one becomes overly tired.

As with Alpine skiing, ski touring should be introduced to the child in short segments. Perhaps, start on a sunny golf course where the child can try out his new skis and gradually build up confidence. More Nordic rentals are becoming available in junior sizes at various touring centers and ski areas which is especially helpful for an Alpine skiing family that has already invested a great deal in downhill equipment but wishes to do some limited touring. As the sport grows, more sizes of Nordic equipment are being carried in your local ski shops.

It is advisable to check on availability of children's Nordic rentals before arriving. Since most of the Nordic equipment is imported the following boot conversion table should prove helpful:

European Size	American Size
28	9 - 10
29	11
30	12
31	13
32	1
33	2
34	3 - 3½

Equipment can be purchased at ski shops, many of which have family, or grow-plans with Nordic equipment as well as Alpine. Used children's skis are often perfect for a young ski tourer. Skis come with both wax or no-wax bases. The proper wax or waxless base (fish-scales or mohair strips) enables the skier to go up hills without sliding backwards but still slide freely while walking on a flat or descending a hill. If wax is required, do not forget to bring an extra supply along. Cross-country skis are normally longer than Alpine skis and the shop or rental personnel can best advise you which length is needed.

Cross-country or ski touring clothing need not be specially purchased as regular Alpine garments or almost any warm, winter clothing is fine. Remember, the child will get warm skiing and cold sitting, so have extra sweaters and a place to carry the discarded layers. Gaiters over the ankles help keep the snow out of the shoes or boots and can be worn well with jeans or knickers.

Guided tours, workshops, and lessons are available at many ski areas and ski touring centers. The Ski Touring Council publishes a detailed guide — "Ski Touring Guide" which describes centers in the United States, tour plans and dates for the season, and gives detailed information on the sport. It can be obtained from:

Ski Touring Council
Troy, Vermont 05868

Further information can also be obtained from the ski areas, the United States Ski Association, your local mountain or ski club, state and national parks, and U.S. Forest Service.

Above all, relax and enjoy the chance to spend a day or afternoon being in the woods with your family and getting good exercise.

Vail photo by Peter Runyon

VI   Competition Skiing

Children are naturally competitive; you need only to spend five or ten minutes at a playground to observe exactly how competitive they are. Competition in a sport can be a very positive, rewarding experience for a child and it is important to carefully investigate the competitive ski program with all aspects of it in mind before enrolling your child. A child can often learn more from competitive skiing than just running a faster slalom, getting more air off the freestyle jumps, or setting a faster pace on a cross-country course. In trying to improve his skiing skills, the young racer in turn becomes aware of his own personal abilities and frequently makes an effort to improve himself as an individual. A child can gain a good deal of maturity and confidence in himself, both physically and emotionally, from participating in a well-run competitive ski program. Furthermore, the contact and shared experiences with other young people his age and level of ability can be most rewarding. Training in a competitive ski program revolves around discipline and self-motivation. Many children benefit more from the strict discipline of a competitive program than from any other aspect and welcome the regulations and boundries.

Competitive skiing should not be forced on an unwilling young skier. It is essential that he wants to race and is willing to commit himself to the program. Before a young skier is enrolled, all aspects of the program should be considered and discussed with the entire family. If the child becomes very active in competitive skiing, families frequently find themselves making many sacrifices in terms of time and expense.

The parent should carefully investigate the program to be sure it is well run and well organized. Valuable ski time should not be lost due to poor organization and planning. I feel a competitive ski program should have strict written rules and guidelines to be adhered to by officials, racers and parents. Well explained rules and procedures only help a program run more smoothly so that everyone knows what is involved, including time, place, and other particulars.

The coach or coaches are definitely key to the program. The coach should be selected not only for his fine technical skiing ability, but also for his ability to relate to young skiers and his interest in them as individuals. A junior ski coach often becomes the idol of his young racers. Hopefully, the coach has the ability to relax and have fun with his team while maintaining control. Training is an essential part of a competitive ski program and should be stressed but never so strongly that the goals and realities of the total program are over-shadowed. I feel a twelve-year-old should be considered first as a twelve-year-old and second as a potential Olympic racer. He should be able to have fun while striving for competitive goals.

If the pressure from the coach and parents becomes too severe, the young racer becomes the real loser. The "Little League Syndrome" is, unfortunately, not lacking in the competitive ski world. You need only stand by the freestyle jumps, the slalom course, the cross-country finish, or the jumping hill, and watch the parents to see how much pressure they exert. It is essential that the parents support their child in his endeavors to compete and win, yet winning should become perhaps secondary to learning, improving, and maturing as an individual and a skier. Parents can support their child without pushing him beyond unrealistic goals.

There is a variety of programs available to young skiers interested in competing. One option is to enroll in the competition or race program at a particular ski area either through its ski club or ski school. These area-sponsored programs differ markedly but usually involve sessions on weekends, occasionally mid-week afternoons, and special training camps during the holidays. Each area and area club often specializes in different events, and the potential competitor and the parents should check the program for his speciality. Some area-sponsored programs, on the other hand, can be very relaxed with races and training only once a week.

Another option is joining a community ski club that sponsors a racing program either at the same area each week or different areas. These ski clubs are usually organized to assist in transportation, offer package deals for their members, and trips. The advantage of a local club is that most of the competitors are from the same area and probably made up of school friends. This certainly helps when car pools are needed to take the racers to the next event or to their weekly training sessions. Also, the local community is often caught up in the excitement and the success of their racers which, while it sometimes puts further pressure on the child, often gives him greater support and recognition for a job well done. Because many of these clubs are run strictly by volunteers and club members, it is important to be sure that they are well organized by serious, dedicated directors, especially when the racers are involved. It is great to have programs run by interested volunteers and family

Photo by Hubert Schriebl; courtesy of Stratton Mountain

members, yet they must realize that they have a responsibility to all members including their racers.

If a young racer is to compete seriously in other than informal club-sponsored events, he will need to become "classified". This means that the racer joins the United States Ski Association, U.S.S.A., and receives a classification card based on his age and, later, his ability. The United States Ski Association is the governing and controlling body in competitive racing. Yet, it is not limited just to competitors; families and individuals can join the U.S.S.A. and receive benefits and opportunities. The U.S.S.A. is made up of seven geographic divisions. While age classifications are standard throughout the Association, certain divisions sponsor varied junior programs in Alpine, Nordic, and freestyle. It is, therefore, important to check with your divisional headquarters as to which junior programs are available in your area. If there is any doubt as to which division you come under, requests can be sent directly to the United States Ski Association, and they will then forward them to your correct division or regional headquarters. A list of the U.S.S.A. divisional headquarters follows:

United States Ski Association
1726 Champa Street, Suite 300
Denver, Colorado 80202

Alaskan Division of U.S.S.A.   *Jurisdiction over the State of Alaska.*
SRA Box 45
Anchorage, Alaska 99507

Central Division - U.S.S.A.   *Jurisdiction over Ohio, Michigan, Indiana,*
P.O. Box 66014   *Illinois, Wisconsin, Minnesota, Iowa, North*
AMF O'Hare   *Dakota, South Dakota, east of the Missouri*
Chicago, Illinois 60666   *River, Missouri (except the counties of Jackson*
                                     and Clay), and Kentucky.

Eastern Division - U.S.S.A.   *Jurisdiction over New England, New York,*
22 High Street   *New Jersey, Pennsylvania, Delaware, Mary-*
Brattleboro, Vt. 05301   *land, District of Columbia, Virginia and West*
                                     Virginia.

Far West Ski Association - U.S.S.A. *Jurisdiction over the States of California, Ari-*
1313 W. 8th St.   *zona and Hawaii, and the State of Nevada with*
Los Angeles, CA 90017   *the exception of the counties of Elko, Eureka,*
                                     and White Pine.

Far West Competition Office - U.S.S.A.
Box BN
Incline Village, NV 89450

Jurisdiction over the States of California, Arizona and Hawaii, and the State of Nevada with the exception of the counties of Elko, Eureka, and White Pine.

Intermountain Division - U.S.S.A.
1431 Terry Drive
Idaho Falls, Idaho 83401

Jurisdiction over the State of Utah and over the Counties of Teton, Sublette, Lincoln, Sweetwater, Fremont and Uinta in Wyoming; and over the following counties in southeastern Idaho: Bannock, Bearl Lake, Bingham, Bonneville, Blaine, Butte, Camas, Caribou, Cassia, Clark, Custer, Franklin, Fremont, Gooding, Jefferson, Jerome, Lemhi, Lincoln, Madison, Mindoka, Oneida, Power, Teton, Twin Falls, and the counties of Elko, Eureka and White Pine in Nevada.

Northern Division of U.S.S.A.
1732 Clark Avenue
Billings, MT 59102

Jurisdiction over the State of Montana, Yellowstone National Park, and in Northern Wyoming the counties of Park, Hot Springs, Bighorn, Washakie, Sheridan, Johnson, Campbell, Crook, Weston, Natrona, and Converse.

Pacific Northwest Division U.S.S.A.
P.O. Box 6228
Seattle, Washington 98188

Jurisdiction over the States of Washington, Oregon, and over the following counties in the State of Idaho: Ada, Adams, Benewah, Boise, Bonner, Boundry, Canyon, Clearwater, Elmore, Gem, Idaho, Kottenai, Latah, Lewis, Nez Perce, Owyhee, Payette, Shoshone, Valley and Washington.

Rocky Mountain Division of U.S.S.A.
1463 Larimer Square
Denver, Colorado 80202

Jurisdiction over the States of Colorado, New Mexico, Nebraska, Kansas, Oklahoma, Texas; the counties of Niobrara, Carbon, Albany, Platte, Goshen, and Laramie in southern Wyoming, South Dakota west of the Missouri River, and the Counties of Jackson and Clay in the State of Missouri.

Southern Division - U.S.S.A.
P.O. Box 801
Belmont, North Carolina 28012

Jurisdiction over Alabama, Arkansas, Florida, Georgia, Louisiana, Mississippi, North Carolina, South Carolina, Puerto Rico, and Tennessee.

One fine junior program that is offered by several of these divisions is known as the Buddy Werner League, named after one of America's finest Alpine skiers. This Alpine team racing program is for junior skiers up to the age of thirteen. It is organized on a low pressure basis with teams made up of racers from a local area. Teams race against other near-by teams within their district and then within their region. If a racer does well within the Buddy Werner League, he often advances to racing in state competitions and eventually to regional and then junior national championships. A very detailed booklet describing this league is available from sponsoring divisions. A similiar junior program is known as the Mighty Mites. Information on each branch of competition, Alpine, Nordic, and freestyle, is available to members from the offices. This information includes schedules, rules, eligibility charts, and training suggestions.

Alpine classification ages:

Junior III - IV: 14 and under

Junior I - II: 14 - 18 years

Freestyle competition is a fairly new development in the skiing field. If a young individual is interested in it, he should keep in close contact with the ski association and freestyle clubs to learn exactly what is available and what new events are being offered.

Freestyle classification ages:

Junior V: 9 and under

Junior IV: 10 - 11 years

Junior III: 12 - 13 years

Junior II: 14 - 15 years

NASTAR at Steamboat; photo courtesy of Portfolio Collection - ATHA

Since safety in freestyle skiing has caused great concern to parents, it is important to know that all U.S.S.A. sponsored meets are held within very strict guidelines at fully patrolled and well equipped ski areas. Freestyle meets usually require participation in four events: stunt ballet, aerials, mogul runs, and compulsory forms. Again, for up-to-date information, a young freestyler should check with his club and regional ski association office.

Nordic competition on the junior level is also fairly new in the U.S. paralleling the general increased interest in cross-country skiing inspired by Bill Koch's winning of a silver medal in the 1976 Olympics. Nordic competition includes both cross-country races and jumping.

Nordic classification ages:

Junior IV: 11 and under

Junior III: 12 - 13 years

Junior II: 14 - 15 years

It is best to write to the regional U.S.S.A. office for the detailed program information and schedules of meets. The Eastern Ski Association, for instance, sponsors a low-key junior Nordic program named for Torger Tokle with local meets similar to the Buddy Werner League.

Torger Tokle classification ages:

Class V: 9 and under.

Class IV: 10 - 11 years

Class III: 11 - 13 years

If a young skier wishes to race only once or twice or race with the entire family and avoid all the U.S.S.A. requirements, NASTAR races are perfect. NASTAR, which stands for *NA*tional *STA*ndard *R*ace, is offered at approximately sixty areas across the United States. The entrant signs up in the morning at a NASTAR registration desk and pays an entry fee of $2.00 to $3.00. NASTAR is an easy giant slalom usually on a smooth, gentle slope at the area. The local pro, or course pace-setter, runs the course each day. Each competitor's time, adjusted for age and sex, is rated against his. Gold, silver or bronze medals are awarded to those who do better than the adjusted standard. If you enter several NASTAR races, you receive a handicap card based on your time, age, and sex as compared with the times of several top pros. The junior NASTAR is sponsored by Pepsi-Cola and the age groups are: six and under, 7 - 9, 10 - 12, 13 - 15, 16 - 18. If the child is six and under and can ski fairly well, his chances of receiving a medal are pretty good. NASTAR results are computerized and therefore are usually available that same afternoon. NASTAR is very relaxed, well run, and fun for the whole family.

Certain areas that do not offer NASTAR races frequently sponsor their own competitions held on a Saturday or Sunday which are equally enjoyable and open to anyone who wishes to sign up.

Relaxed family racing is available and fun. It is important to remember that even when racing in NASTAR or just a club race, pressuring a child is usually counter-productive.

5, 4, 3, 2, 1, Go! Relax, ski well, and have fun.

VII

Where to Ski

Deciding where to ski is always one of the major questions, and the decision can be crucial. The choice of an area with the right sort of children's facilities can make the difference between children liking or disliking skiing and thus the parents having a good or bad time as well.

Most families seem to depend upon grapevine information from friends and friends of friends who have skied at a certain area which, unfortunately, is not always accurate. There exists a wide variety of facilities and ski programs for children at the many ski areas across the U.S. and Canada. Some areas are extremely well equipped for families and well planned to accommodate children's special needs, while others are lacking. Certain areas claiming to be "family areas" are, in reality, very poorly set up for the younger members.

It is important to know as much about an area as possible before packing up the kids. It does help to talk with other families who have skied there with the understanding that their opinions may be based entirely on personal circumstances. Area brochures can help but some are apt to be full of pretty color pictures of children skiing when the area is not at all geared to children. Also, ski areas as a whole are very slow at sending requested information so start investigating possible places well in advance. Many areas have toll free numbers which are useful for checking possible changes in times, costs and availability of certain services and programs.

If you have only one area nearby and feel that the children's facilities and programs are sorely lacking, it doesn't hurt to contact the management and express your concern and desires. If several families back a proposal for increased children's programs, it will carry a lot more weight.

Photo by Bill Forsyth; courtesy of Bromley Mountain

I have been fortunate to have had my children with me on most of my trips to various ski areas which, by putting one in the ski school and one in the nursery, allowed me to get a fairly complete picture of the facilities and programs. The following criteria became important to me for judging various areas and will hopefully prove helpful to you, as parents, in making choices among different areas. Since each family has different concerns, there undoubtedly are factors in my selection process that will be less important to others.

NURSERY

1. Your child must be the right age since many nurseries have age restrictions.
2. The nursery hours should be geared to ski lift hours.
3. Lunch should be provided or there should be a nursery staff to feed children bringing their own lunches. If lunch is not provided, the schedule for parents to pick up the child should be somewhat flexible and at the parents' convenience. If the area is very large, lunch pick-up proves a real and unnecessary hassle.
4. The nursery should be well staffed and well run with printed rates, rules, and procedures. Parents should have to sign children in and out and include medical information and such things as home and local addresses on the sign-in sheet.
5. The nursery facility should be well-equipped with sturdy toys, cribs, bathrooms, and some kitchen facilities.
6. A maximum number of children acccepted should be set, based on the size and staff of the nursery.
7. Ideally, out-door play should be provided.
8. The staff should refuse obviously sick children to protect the healthy ones.

PRE-SKI SCHOOL OR NURSERY SKI SCHOOL

1. If you have a three-, four-, or five-year-old who is interested in skiing, you should select an area that has a pre-ski school.
2. A pre-ski school should have specially trained instructors and ideally no more than five little children per instructor.
3. The teaching area should be a short walk from the nursery.
4. Emphasis should be, first, on having fun on skis and, second, on technique.
5. Ideally, the instructor should pick up and deliver the child at the nursery.

CHILDREN'S SKI SCHOOL

1. Special children's classes with specially trained instructors (who hopefully are not all girls) should be offered.
2. The children's ski school should have its own meeting and teaching area.
3. There should never be more than ten children per class.
4. The majority of ski-school time should be spent skiing and not in listening to long lectures on technique. Also valuable ski-school time should not be lost in organizing and assembling the classes.
5. All-day programs with supervised lunch should be available at larger areas.

6. All ability levels of special children's instruction from beginner to advanced or racing should be offered.

THE AREA IN GENERAL

1. The facilities and services should be centrally located and easy for children and parents to find without long walks between various locations.

2. Children's discount lift tickets and sometimes discount ski school lessons should be available.

3. The area should be family-oriented with such helpful extras as lift operators who automatically slow the lifts down for children.

4. Families should look for a relaxed family atmosphere as opposed to a fast, "jet-set" environment. Your children will definitely have more ski pals and children of the same age and ability in their classes at a family area.

5. Families might look for extras such as children's ski-week parties and children's fun races.

Unfortunately, since there are few ideal areas, parents have to be somewhat flexible and, in turn, set up their own family priorities. If you are arriving by car, plan to unload the children as near the base area as possible before parking. If you plan to stay at an area or nearby lodge, consider non-skiing activities such as swimming, sleigh rides, and game rooms. There is more to a ski trip than just being on skis.

On the following pages I have briefly described twenty-five areas I have visited which will hopefully provide a helpful guideline to you as parents. I only regret I wasn't able to go to more areas. The Area Directory at the end of the book compiled from data supplied by the areas themselves should also prove helpful, but as times, costs and programs are constantly changing, it is wise to double check. The opening sections concentrate on Aspen, Colorado and a few other special well-known areas in North America, though I do not necessarily suggest that they are a must for all families. However, they do represent what any prominent and popular area does or doesn't provide.

Area Hopping: Although skiing different areas can be lots of fun and offer variety, it is important to remember that young children seem to do better when they are on familiar ground with the same smiling ski instructor and classmates each day. Also, ski school and lift prices for several days are usually more economical. If children feel at home, they relax and learn faster.

If you area-hop, be sure the ski schools teach a relatively similar technique. Even with the same method, different classes, ski school procedures, and terrain distract the child somewhat from learning. Once they are older and fairly confident skiers they will adjust better and area hopping can be more fun. Even though areas are joined in a group with interchangeable tickets, the mountain facilities and important locations can all be very different.

ASPEN, COLORADO

There are so many ways to consider Aspen that it is hard to know where to begin. Aspen is a fascinating and exciting resort town surrounded by four fabulous ski areas with super skiing for all levels of ability. Whether you are beating through the steep moguls on the back of Bell Mountain, silently following the cross-country trails through a great open valley at Ashcroft, trying out the Graduated Length Method (GLM) at Highlands, skiing the fluffy powder on the Big Burn at Snowmass, or watching your child enter a children's race at Buttermilk, skiing is what Aspen is all about in winter. The town alone is fascinating with its old, Colorado mining-town buildings and many attractive shops and restaurants.

In contrast to its fast reputation, Aspen can be a great spot for a family ski vacation. However, because it is spread out and the pace is often hectic, a family ski trip to Aspen takes a lot of pre-planning, organization and patience, the rewards of which are great skiing and plenty of fun for all.

Of the four separate ski areas, three are run by the Aspen Skiing Corporation; Highlands is separately owned and managed. Lift tickets, however, are interchangeable so you can try each area. Aspen Mountain, locally called "Ajax", rises directly above the town and lifts are only a short walk from many lodges. Buttermilk and Highlands are both about fifteen minutes out of town, and Snowmass, with its own village, is about thirty minutes away. Since traffic can be bad, these time estimates can vary, but shuttle buses are available. Unless your family is staying at Snowmass, however, I feel having a car is practically essential and definitely helpful for picking up children from nurseries and ski school.

All Aspen nurseries are privately owned and operated in a variety of locations both in and out of town. At Snowmass, however, both "Kinderheim" locations are within walking distance from most condominiums and inns. I have included a list, on page 74 , of some of the nurseries available but check ahead because Aspen has had a history of a great turnover in their nursery and day-care centers. An up-to-date list of nurseries can also be obtained by writing the Chamber of Commerce. Aspen is a "reservations only" town so be prepared to make reservations in advance for nurseries and ski rentals. For evening babysitting, the girls who work at the lodges are often available and anxious to earn the extra spending money. Two dollars an hour seemed to be the going rate. Also, when writing to stores or nurseries, be careful to include the correct box number; the Aspen post office loves to stamp "return to sender".

Aspen has really never stopped growing and as a result, activities are available to suit most every interest. In addition to Nordic and Alpine skiing, Sno-cat tours, snowmobiling, tennis, ice skating, sleigh and dog sled rides, art exhibits, a library, movies, game rooms, shops, and all sorts of restaurants are there to be enjoyed. Night life in Aspen is certainly hard to beat.

Information can be acquired from:
The Aspen Chamber of Commerce
Wheeler Opera House
328 E. Hyman Ave.
Aspen, Colo. 81611

Aspen Mountain

There are no two ways about it, Aspen Mountain, or "Ajax", offers fantastic skiing. It is mostly an intermediate to expert mountain, and with fresh powder, the back of Bell Mountain, part of the same complex, is hard to match. Although a good little skier could handle the terrain, it might be stretching the family finances. There are no children's rates on Aspen Mountain and no children's ski school. The Aspen Ski School holds all children's classes at Buttermilk and Snowmass. Parents meet their ski school classes up on the mountain in front of Gretle's great restaurant.

It is very possible to enroll your child in the children's ski school at nearby Buttermilk and then go back and ski on Ajax. Just be sure to allow enough time to ski down and drive to Buttermilk to pick up your child after his class. Traffic in and around Aspen after skiing can get pretty heavy. While parking around the base of the mountain is very scarce, area shuttle buses or lodge services are available and Aspen Good Time Guides offers a children's ski school delivery and pick-up service. This really helps parents who are skiing on Aspen Mountain allowing them to take that extra run and not fight the traffic.

For super skiing for parents or older, advanced kids, Ajax is hard to beat. Highlands, Buttermilk, and Snowmass are, however, more suitable areas for most children.

Buttermilk

Buttermilk is a great ski school mountain with beautiful beginner slopes and even some expert trails. The kids can easily find pals to ski with or play with after ski school. Children's classes meet daily at 9:00 in a special meeting place. Unfortunately, the assembling and sorting-out process is extremely chaotic and there are many confused and bewildered parents but somehow, before you know it, everyone is in a class and off they go. The children, who eat lunch with their instructors, must have lunch money (at least $1.00) with them. At 3:00 p.m., ski school is dismissed and children are allowed to ski on the T-bar only until their parents arrive. One ski instructor is always there until the last parents straggle back from Ajax or wherever. Also, there is a ski school representative assigned to take care of the child who is not feeling well, or is extremely tired or cold. She usually takes him into the ski school office to watch the gerbil or the restaurant to sip cocoa.

The instructors under the supervision of Linda Harland (Bullwinkel) all have great nicknames: Gorilla, Radar, Potatoes, and Sarge and appear to love teaching children. Also, there seems to be a good ratio of men teaching as well. Although there is no special children's teaching area, there is plenty of room and a perfect beginners slope with a T-bar right by the base lodge. Parents can sit on the balcony and proudly watch their little ones descend. Since the whole area is geared to teaching, the lifts and runs are manageable. The more advanced "hot-shot" skiers can be easily challenged by the expert slopes; it isn't just a beginners' area. Children have a place at Buttermilk, almost as if it were their own area, and they find their way around easily. There are three separate parking areas: Buttermilk West, Tiehack, and main Buttermilk. Families should head to the main Buttermilk parking area, located right near the Holiday Inn, since the children's ski school and rental shop are there. Be careful not to end up at the wrong parking area on your last run down, however.

For the three- through six-year-old group, a new program called the Aspen Pre-School Hot Dog Clinic is available. This privately run clinic is basically an all-day program for children too young for the ski school. The parents meet the clinic staff in the Buttermilk cafeteria, and the staff skis with the children in the morning and afternoon. They have special events such as a gingerbread race, a photographer to catch the kids in action, or a trip to have a Kentucky Fried Chicken lunch. The parents do not have to be skiing at Buttermilk but must list their location on the sign-in form. This is a new program which hopefully will continue and expand as the need is definitely there.

Snowmass

Snowmass is a family area and quite centralized for those staying there. The condominiums, lodges, shops, and restaurants are clustered along the side of the ski slope and lifts are a short way on skis from most doors. For non-skiers or small children, be prepared to climb a lot of stairs because Snowmass Village is built on a hill. If you are arriving by car for a day of skiing with children, don't hesitate to ask the parking attendants where to park, as it is confusing. If you have three- through six-year-olds for the Kinderheim, be sure you park in the village area or as close as possible. If you arrive by the Shuttle Bus, there is no

The Snowmass ski school functions on the same plan as Buttermilk as it operates under the Aspen Ski School and Aspen Ski Corporation. Children's classes with lunch supervision are available for six- through twelve-year-olds. Yet, if the parents are influential, the six-year-old cut off age can apparently be flexible. The ski school is large with about forty-seven qualified special instructors under a fine supervisor, Peter Dahl. The prevailing attitude of the school is that children should have fun and they certainly seem to. During holidays and peak vacation periods, however, the ski school classes can be much too large with more than ten children in a class. Because of terrain and space, the ski school meeting place for children and beginners at the Village Mall is crowded and can be confusing. Also, the children's teaching area is not at all ideal and not separated from what is happening on the beginners slope - Fanny Hill. Once the children are more advanced and up higher on the mountain, they have more space. Both children and parents have plenty of chances for great skiing as Snowmass offers a wide variety of terrain and plenty of slopes.

For the three- through six-year-old crowd, Grace and Bruce Oliphant seem to have a super program, the Kinderheim. The Kinderheim has two locations, one at the Inns of Snowmass and one on the bottom level of the Silver Tree Inn. This is an outdoor oriented program, for which children supply their own ski equipment, with the basic goal of teaching the smaller fry to ski. Yet, in addition to the skiing, they have marvelous crafts, good play equipment, puppet shows, stories, and rest periods. It is a well organized, well structured program and both locations are very cheery and well designed. All children are organized into "color groups" according to their skiing ability and all their equipment is marked with colored tape indicating their group. For further identification, they wear Kinderheim ski bibs, a definite plus in my mind. There is one instructor for each group of five children. They also have special fenced-off areas for skiing decorated with cut-out figures including a dragon. However, the upper Kinderheim at the Silver Tree seemed to offer a better slope.

Both are very conveniently located close to the nurseries and are basically ski playgrounds. I did feel however they could use more area with better terrain, where children could do more than one turn at a time. If your children are in the Kinderheim, they will be well taken care of, get a good introduction to skiing, and have lots of fun; and that's what counts.

Child care, for those from two to twelve, in Snowmass is also available at the Village Child Care Center or by specially pre-arranged baby-sitters. Since there is a great turnover in Aspen nurseries, check ahead. The Village Child Care Center is located in Snowmass down the road from the Village Center. Since I was unable to find it, I have to advise that you call ahead for good directions.

There are lots and lots of children at Snowmass and plenty of non-skiing activities such as sleigh rides, swimming, and game rooms. In addition, good ski touring is available. Since shuttle buses run regularly to and from Aspen, you can easily stay there, about twenty minutes away, and ski at Snowmass.

Aspen Highlands

Highlands is a lovely, large area with twelve lifts, the longest vertical drop in Colorado, and great slopes. While it is independent of the Aspen Skiing Corporation, the same lift tickets can be used. It also has its own shuttle buses and ski school. The beginning teaching area, with the "Half-inch" poma lift and wide gentle slopes known as "Mother's" and "Apple Pie", is located directly across from the base lodge. For experts, runs like "The Wall", "Moment of Truth", and "Lower Stein" will certainly keep your knees in shape and blood circulating, and for the scenery seekers, the view from "Lodges Peak" lift up to the 11,800 foot summit can't be matched - it is spectacular.

Currently, there is no nursery at Highlands, yet plans are being considered to make it an area for the whole family. There are special classes for children five years old and up; all day classes with lunch supervision are provided. The main emphasis of the Highland's ski school is G.L.M. (Cliff Taylor's direct parallel method). However, good non-G.L.M. classes are equally available. Children are taught in separate classes especially adapted to their special needs, and during holidays they have a separate enclosed teaching area. By comparison, the children's classes seemed smaller than at Buttermilk and Snowmass. The whole area and ski school are relaxed and low key.

Along with some great terrain and excellent skiing for all ability levels, Highlands also offers NASTAR races and freestyle activity. The Merry-Go-Round Restaurant up on the mountain is a delightful, attractive spot to relax and eat lunch. Also, the base lodge certainly comes alive about 3:30 or 4:00 with two bands and plenty of excitement and fun.

Aspen Information

For an up to date list of Aspen child care facilities write:

Aspen Chamber of Commerce
Wheeler Opera House
328 East Hyman Ave.
Aspen, Colo. 81611

Reservations are recommended at all Day Care facilities such as:

Aspen Good Time Guides, 4 months and up - daily and evenings - chaperone service, bring your own lunch: Box 1624, tel. 925-4661

Aspen Pre-School Hot Dog Clinic, 3-6 years old, daily ski program - lunch included: Buttermilk, tel. 925-7120

Happy Face Montessori Children's Center, 2½ and up, daily - lunch included: Box 11019, tel. 925-6444

Hobbit House, 2½ - 6, daily - lunch included: Box 9229, tel. 925-5347

Kinderheim, 3-6 years old, daily - lunch included: Snowmass, Box 5446, tel. 923-3175

The Village Child Care Center, 2-12 years old, daily - lunch included: Snowmass, Box 5254, tel. 923-4200

VAIL, COLORADO

Vail is really the "milk and honey land" of children's skiing. It is one of the few areas to realize that a child of five years and up in ski school for one week needs to be entertained as well as taught. The children in the Vail ski school learn a lot and have so much fun that parents can go off and ski, knowing everyone is happy.

In my opinion, Vail's children's ski school is definitely one of the best. The children meet at either Lions Head or Golden Peak and new children are efficiently and quickly assigned to the proper classes, either by age for first time beginners, or age and ability for chair lift skiers. The classes usually stay together from day to day so children become well acquainted with each other and their instructor. Shortly after meeting, the classes are off for the day to ski hard and discover the fun and surprises Vail has in store for them. One fantastic children's spot is Peanut Peak, a specially enclosed children's ski playground with obstacle courses, roller coaster bumps, games, an igloo with a cocoa machine inside, and its own poma lift. A smaller enclosed terrain-garden or ski playground is at the Golden Peak base. Also on the mountain there are special treats such as an Indian Tepee, a Miner's Shaft, and a maze through the woods. Classes eat lunch with their instructors either in a reserved children's room at Lions Head, in town, or on a picnic. Thursday is children's ski school race day with ribbons for all. The Bratskeller provides supervision before and after ski school. Again there are two locations at Golden Peak and Lions Head, a great added service for parents. The children's ski school is very safety conscious as it is on a big mountain. Supervisors are constantly in touch with radios and if a child is not feeling well, he is usually escorted down the mountain by a Vail hostess and returned to the supervised Bratskeller. Children's ski school director, Hadley Gray, is determined to see that children are well cared for, learn to ski, and have fun.

Nursery facilities are at the Small World Nursery above the Vail Clinic and a shuttle bus ride or long hike away from the lifts. The nursery is adequately equipped and does have plenty of space. There is a maximum of forty, so plan to be early over holiday periods. Lunch is included and ski lessons with equipment are available on a small, somewhat pathetic hill behind the nursery. The children learn some, have fun, and above all get outside.

Vail photo by Peter Runyon

Compared with the excellent ski school program for the older children, this program, especially the hill, is somewhat lacking. The four-year-old who can ski well is sadly without a program, other than hiring a special babysitter to ski with him.

If you are arriving at Vail for the first time, head straight to the information center and orient yourself. Vail has grown rapidly and is very spread out but a shuttle bus connects most facilities. In addition to Alpine and Nordic skiing, ice skating, tennis, swimming, and great stores and restaurants are available. Vail is big but it is well run and very manageable for a family.

STEAMBOAT, COLORADO

If you want to see lots of young children singing, laughing, and skiing high up on Mount Werner, Steamboat is the place. It is amazing to see how quickly these great instructors, under Ronnie Connley's careful supervision, manage to get the children skiing and up to the upper slopes via the gondola. It is not at all unusual to see a Gondola car arriving with six pairs of small skis in the holders and six tiny heads peaking out the windows. There are a lot of children skiing at Steamboat, and it is understandable because the program is good and the mountain is fantastic for kids and parents alike. The only thing really lacking is a special children's teaching area. They do share a slope and a pony lift with beginning adults, but it is protected from other skiers.

The nursery, on the lower level of the Gondola Building, is well run under the direction of a real pro, Joyce Kittle, and amply staffed and equipped with plenty of toys, four separate crib rooms, and a lunch room for the three- through six-year-old skiers. Children under three must be picked up for lunch, because there are no facilities to feed this younger group. They will, however, refrigerate baby food. This can be a nuisance, but parents can hop right back on the gondola, with no lines, to get back up. The Kiddie Corral ski nursery runs from 10:00-3:00 with supervised lunch. Nursery supervision prior to and after ski school can also be arranged for six- and seven-year-olds. Children ages six through twelve are known as the "Rough Riders". Both "Kiddie Corral" and "Rough Rider" ski school children wear ski bibs in a Western motif with their names which aids in keeping track of all ski school children. The "Rough Riders" have a special meeting place at stakes marked - "Billy Kidd", "Calamity Jane", "Doc Holiday", etc. which indicate their ability level. Since they are reclassified every day, they unfortunately don't seem to stay with the same class or instructor long. Yet, those children that can do snowplow turns are quickly in the gondola, which alone is exciting, heading up the mountain where they ski and have lunch with their instructor. They get a lot of mileage out of their skiing, the classes are not too big, and the instructors, many of them young men, are very professional children's instructors. The children learn to ski, learn to run slalom gates, and have fun.

In addition to Alpine skiing, cross-country, sleigh rides, swimming and tennis are all available. The town is about two miles from the ski area and offers more shopping, including a marvelous old-fashioned western store - F.M. Light & Sons. Also, if you want more skiing, night skiing is available at Howelsen Hill. Thus it is easy to understand why Steamboat is known as "Ski Town, U.S.A." It is a relaxed, enjoyable family area.

Photo courtesy of Steamboat

"SKI THE SUMMIT", COLORADO

Keystone, Breckenridge, Copper Mountain and A-Basin are four areas located in Summit County, Colorado which have united to offer interchangeable lift packages. Visitors can stay at one of the areas or in the nearby towns of Frisco, Dillon or Silverthorn, and ski at all the areas.

As a result, however, the areas are catering more to a daily trade rather than "ski week" programs. The number of children in ski school or the nursery varies greatly from day to day, and it is hard to compare their programs with other areas dealing with children who are usually at an area for five days.

Keystone

Keystone is a very attractive, well laid out area surrounded by beautiful mountains and a spectacular view of both the Gore and Ten Mile Ranges. The slopes and trails are well maintained, and there are few moguls to deter young skiers. However, "Last Hoot", in full view of the base lodge, does provide plenty of thrills for the expert. Families should not be concerned at the first sight of this steep trail because on the upper part of the mountain are smooth, open, beginner and intermediate trails.

The base lodge, known as the Mountain House, is definitely the center of activities. There are three floors with a nursery, ski and rental shop, ski school and ticket offices, ski patrol, and eating and bar facilities. Upstairs, families congregate on comfortable living room couches which look out onto the slopes. These certainly beat hard wooden benches found in some base lodges.

The nursery, located on the ground floor of the Mountain House, is bright and cheery with big windows and fun equipment. Cribs are available in a separate room. Reservations are required for children under two and suggested for all children. Unfortunately, like so many ski nurseries, it could easily become overcrowded. In connection with the nursery and ski school, Lynn Jones runs a nursery ski program for children three years old and up. Children must provide their own equipment however and small size equipment is very scarce at the Mountain House rental shop. The children have ski lessons and snow play in both the morning and afternoon and return to the nursery for lunch and supervision. Older children or nursery children who are better skiers may also take advantage of the nursery facilities and lunch while joining the regular ski school for morning and afternoon sessions. Both schools meet very near the base lodge, a short walk for children carrying equipment. Although Lynn Jones seems to do a marvelous job and has an unending amount of patience, there were too many young beginners per instructor. Also, as there was no separate children's teaching area, the young tots were instructed at the bottom of the beginner's slope which is not ideal.

Like other summit ski areas, ski school attendance greatly fluctuates which makes setting up expanded children's programs difficult. In the regular ski school, both children and adults meet together in the same area. The atmosphere is chaotic and confusing for both parents and children. If the children are more advanced skiers, they often end up in a predominently adult class because, although Keystone attempts to keep all children

Photo courtesy of Keystone International, Colorado

together, there is often not enough demand for children's classes on the higher levels. Hopefully, the area will be able to expand its children's program and provide a special children's teaching area, more classes, and a meeting place.

For families skiing together, Keystone offers wide, gentle slopes but beware of fast chair lifts and insist that the operator slow the lift down for small children.

Also, the nearby condominium area, Keystone Village Plaza, houses John Gardner's tennis center, and offers swimming, dog sled rides, and sleigh rides. Keystone takes advantage of its beautiful Rocky Mountain setting and extensive ski touring with ski rentals, instruction, and trails. It is a fine family place and hopefully, with expanded children's ski school facilities, it will soon become a great area for all ages.

Breckenridge

Breckenridge is a pretty area that actually encompasses two interconnecting peaks - Peak 8 and Peak 9, both with base lodges and ski school meeting areas. Peak 9's base is only a block or two from the center of town and Peak 8's base is a short drive up the hill from town. The Breckenridge peaks offer excellent family skiing with many wide open, gentle slopes.

Nursery facilities, located in both Peak 8 and Peak 9 base lodges, accept all ages with no maximum so the facilities can easily become overcrowded. They do have cable T.V. and a good crafts program which helps keep little ones happy, but be prepared for quite a crowd. A nursery ski program is available for the three- through six-year-old group at Peak 8 with children providing their own equipment. They are taught in a protected area on the beginner's slope but it, unfortunately, is a long walk from the nursery. If nursery age children are good skiers, they can be accepted into the regular ski school on the nursery ski instructor's recommendation. No all day supervision is available for children's ski school or nursery which, at Peak 8, does not prove too difficult since all eating facilities are at the base. On Peak 9, the trip down to the nursery is more inconvenient especially since there is a mountain summit restaurant. The ski school, under the direction of Hans Garger, seemed well run, and children do meet in their own area with special children's instructors. There were as many male instructors as female, and the children all seemed to be happy, having fun, and in good hands.

Breckenridge has a great relaxed family atmosphere and the wide, smooth trails are perfect for young skiers gaining confidence. The town is a picturesque old mining town and, although the area has developed, it is still contained. It is also reasonably inexpensive.

Copper Mountain

Copper Mountain has become well known as a family ski area, and has earned its reputation. The few lodges and condominiums are nestled at the foot of the mountain a short walk from the lift. The area is very well run and family oriented with several children's programs. For children five through twelve years old, an all day program is available with cocoa breaks and indoor games if blizzards are howling. The children meet in a special separate area and are divided by age and ability into small classes with special instructors.

For the six- through ten-year-olds, there is a Mini Freestyle Racing Team on a semi-seasonal basis. These little kids really ski and learn. The Copper Choppers, eight- through eighteen-year-olds, meet every Saturday or Sunday for ten weeks with Denver transportation available. Children's programs are given top priority.

The Child Center, conveniently located in the base lodge near the ticket windows, is roomy, very well designed and run, with lots of crafts and toys. However, it might be advisable to drop off children by the base lodge before parking, especially on weekends.

Copper offers a lot of skiing; don't be deceived by what you see from the road as you are only getting a glimpse. It has great, long, gentle beginner trails as well as some expert slopes which offer perfect race terrain with many sanctioned amateur, junior, and professional races. Copper also has long slopes that families of varied ability can ski together.

For the cross-country, ski touring advocates, the great glacial valley in which the base of the area is located, offers marvelous cross-country trails, including twelve miles of marked tours starting at the base lodge. There is also a cross-country program for children, which is an unusual bonus.

As Copper is conveniently located and an easy drive from Denver, it can get very crowded on weekends. Yet, it does have a good lift capacity and great open bowls for future expansion.

A-Basin

I usually think of A-Basin on warm muggy days in May, when you know that, high up in the Rockies, skiers are swishing down corn-snow slopes and basking in the sun and clear, cool air. A-Basin is not just a spring skiing mecca, but a great place to ski all season long, and it is a long season.

A-Basin offers good, varied terrain with a lovely wide teaching slope, real thrillers, like "Palivacinni", and wonderful open bowls. Yet, it is high, 12,500 feet at the summit, and 10,800 feet at the base. If you are not used to a higher elevation, take your time adjusting and remember children can be very bothered by altitude. Also, don't plan to take children to the top on cold, windy days. The upper bowls are above the timber line and can be unbearably cold for everyone, especially the younger skiers.

Although I have not visited the nursery, all reports are that it is well run and well equipped. Special children's ski school classes are available, but, because of less demand during the week, your child might not find too many pals of his own age and skiing ability. Yet the smaller crowds certainly help with lift lines.

On a warm sunny day, A-Basin can provide beautiful family skiing, but count on a trip to the base to pick up the nursery child for lunch and to rejoin the ski school child. A-Basin is a delightful place to ski, relaxed and very friendly.

WINTER PARK, COLORADO

It is always hard not to be biased towards one's "home" ski area. Yet, Winter Park has been a special place for me and the multitudes of children who learned to ski here.

Once known as West-Portal, Winter Park has a rich railroad history as well as it's ski history. In addition, Winter Park is blessed with fantastic terrain, excellent exposure, beautiful scenery, and a good average snowfall. Although the summit is 11,025 feet, the slopes are well sheltered and protected by trees. Winter Park has long been a leader in slope maintenance and grooming; even in lean snow years, the slopes are kept in the best possible condition. Winter Park and its challenging new area, Mary Jane, with mostly expert and intermediate slopes, provides the kind of variety to be found on some 400 skiable acres with 13 lifts and 51 slopes and trails.

Winter Park has always been associated with children's skiing and for several generations, children have come by train, bus, or car, in groups or with their families, to learn to ski. It is definitely a family area, and the management has made a great effort to accommodate children. The lift operators are fantastic at slowing down the chair lifts for children without being asked. Both base areas, Winter Park and Mary Jane, are well centralized. However, if a child ended up at Winter Park instead of Mary Jane, it could pose problems. The nursery is bright, cheery and extremely well equipped with separate crib rooms, toys and play equipment. It is organized, well run, and well staffed. The only draw-back is that no lunch is provided and parents must return to pick up their children at mid-day. Since the mountain is so big, this can prove to be a real problem. An all-day nursery ski school program with lunch is available however, for children five through eight years old. Unfortunately, there is no pre-school ski school.

The children's ski school is well organized. Children five through seven years old meet at their own enclosed hill and rope tow, Mount Glenda, which is conveniently located between the warming house and ski shop. The older eight- through twelve-year-olds meet nearby at another enclosed hill, Mount Maury. Children who have skied before are placed in their ability-level classes by performing one or two turns on these hills. In my opinion, this is often not enough to judge the child's skiing ability which in turn can lead to his being placed in the wrong class. Also, be sure your child's poles are well marked as children below the parallel level are taught without poles and leave them at the meeting place. (I personally feel poles should be used earlier, and long walks or lift lines without poles can prove very frustrating for children). Winter Park has several specially trained girls who are great at teaching children to ski, and the enclosed teaching areas are super. If you have a handicapped child, Winter Park is unique in that it offers special ski classes which are marvelous. They even occasionally run a NASTAR race for the handicapped.

Overnight, with the development of Mary Jane, Winter Park has become a major ski area. It will probably require some readjusting before all area facilities catch up to its new size. Winter Park has always been well run, and I'm sure will continue to be. Yet, as it grows, new and more expanded programs, such as children's ski classes with all day supervision and a pre-school ski school, will hopefully be added. It is my wish that before long, parents and children in ski school will no longer have to return to the base to meet at noon time or pick up a brother or sister at the nursery for lunch.

Most of the lodges and motels are about two miles away in Hideway Park. Shuttle bus service is provided by the lodges. Other activities include snowmobile tours and good ski touring. Ski touring centers with trails and rentals for the whole family are located at Beaver's Chalet in Hideway Park and Devil's Thumb Ranch in Fraser.

SNOWBIRD, UTAH

Snowbird is usually thought of as an "expert only" mountain. Although the area is known for its challenging and thrilling deep powder skiing, there are several great trails for young skiers and beginners. Snowbird is not a family ski area by comparison to many others; yet, as more and more avid skiers and "powder hounds" bring their children along, these families are rapidly finding that good terrain and ski instruction for children is available. "Big Emma", a super wide slope, is a delight for any skier young and old, expert and novice.

Another great advantage to Snowbird is that the lodges, shops and restaurants, and the tram are all within a short walk of each other. There is an extremely friendly atmosphere with plenty of Western hospitality. It is a well planned and beautifully developed area.

Ski school director Junior Bounous has done much to make children's classes special and fun. A good program with all day instruction and supervision is available, which is essential on such a big mountain. There is a good short chair lift called "Chickadee" close by the area base center which provides fine skiing for young children or beginners. The ski school also hosts parties for their classes. At one such party, an eight year old girl was seen in tears because she did not want to say good-bye to her class and instructor.

If you are staying in one of the lodges, free babysitting is offered in a bright, cheery room in the Cliff Lodge. Children four years old and up are accepted and the room is well equipped. Yet, the service may be changing so be sure to check.

If it's super skiing you want, some of the best I've ever had, then Snowbird is the place.

PARK CITY, UTAH

Park City caters especially to children of all ages and has great children's ski programs. It is a well planned and conveniently laid out area with lovely wide open slopes and that great Utah powder. The U.S. Ski Team's National Training Center is also headquartered at Park City.

The nursery, known as the "Kinderhaus" is by the base complex in a separate building with a fenced in yard for outside play. It is not only picturesque but well equipped and run. The nursery accepts children of all ages and offers a nourishing hot lunch. There is a limit of forty, with restrictions on the number of babies, so plan to make reservations. Children three through six can participate in a super nursery ski program either for one session or all day. The instructor also leaves the parent a note describing the child's progress, which is a most helpful and thoughtful addition.

For children six through twelve years old, an all day supervised ski school program is available. Since the mountain is big, this program helps free parents from having to return to the base for lunch. Children's classes are kept small and manageable with six children the usual number per instructor which is a good ratio. Park City is also planning a "ski playground" (terrain garden) to further expand their children's facilities and emphasize the fun

Photo courtesy of Snowbird

side of skiing. Families seem to head for Park City all season long so your children will find plenty of new ski buddies. Also, there is a shop in town called Kindersport that sells and rents only children's equipment and clothing. In fact, it has ski boots as small as children's size 6 and can even outfit two-year-olds.

Park City was once an old mining town and the image has remained. However, now snow or "white gold" seems more abundant in the beautiful Wasatch mountains than real gold. The whole family will enjoy the relaxed, friendly atmosphere at Park City and I definitely recommend it.

SUN VALLEY, IDAHO

When it comes to skiing with children, Sun Valley is almost in a class by itself. Although the two mountains, Baldy and Dollar are a short drive from the lodging complex of Sun Valley, or the town of Ketchum, Idaho, an excellent shuttle bus service is available. This is one of the oldest ski areas in the country with years of experience serving skiing families. There are over fifty-eight miles of trails and truly excellent skiing is available.

For the nursery group, Sun Valley's fine Playschool is available. The Playschool is a well equipped rambling little house at the end of the Sun Valley Mall with a playroom, ski room, and separate crib rooms. Special Nursery Ski School instruction is available. Playschool ski instructors take the children, with their specially numbered racing bibs, via shuttle bus to Dollar for instruction and then back to the Playschool for lunch. If the children wish, they can return for afternoon skiing or for other activities such as ice skating or organized games. The most shy babies seemed happy to be there. The Playschool will also provide babysitting at the lodges or during the evenings by prior arrangement.

The regular children's ski school is also excellent. Children meet either at Dollar or on top of Baldy depending upon their ability. The Baldy kids are pretty good advanced little skiers so check with the ski school first as to where to send your child. Morning and afternoon sessions with lunch supervision are available, which is especially important since many children are at Dollar, while their parents are skiing on Baldy. There is a children's ski school representative whose only job is to check on such problems as children being too cold, without lunch money, or too tired. The children's ski school has a special meeting area but surprisingly no "terrain garden" or "ski playground." However, they have ski school races with prizes for all.

There is a great atmosphere at Sun Valley, and it is a beautiful area, though it is not inexpensive. Budget plenty. Also, Sun Valley seems reluctant to send requested information so don't hesitate to use their toll-free number and pursue your requests. I definitely recommend Sun Valley as a fantastic place to take the whole family.

MOUNT SNOW, VERMONT

Mount Snow is a large area with ample facilities where the area management has attempted to cater to skiers of all ages and abilities. As with many Eastern ski areas, Mount Snow has its own unique group of regulars and seems to be especially popular with families and ski clubs from the New York area who are enrolled in ski week programs.

Children, very important and welcome at Mount Snow, have their own picturesque nursery building known as the Pumpkin Patch located next to the base lodge. In spite of being well run by Nancy Alfara and well equipped with plenty of toys, it is overcrowded. A fine nursery ski school program is available for children. Both nursery ski school and the regular children's ski school use Piperville, the children's teaching area and ski playground, which has specially contoured slopes, a 250-foot rope tow, and obstacle courses. Piperville became identified with Mt. Snow's former tall man on skis, Rudi Wyrsch. Children could ski between his stilt legs and loved it. Piperville is an enjoyable place and an ideal area for learning to ski. Under program director Tom Montemagni, a special children's ski week schedule has been developed with races, parties, and a real highlight—video tape sessions. The parents seemed to enjoy it and benefit as much as the children.

In addition to skiing, Mount Snow offers ice skating on an indoor rink in the base lodge and swimming in a heated pool outside the base lodge. Yet, with so much going on, young children can easily get lost in the shuffle, so be sure to set up meeting places. The eighteen lifts and fifty-five trails offer plenty of skiing for everyone and unfortunately on weekends, it seems as if everyone is there. During the week or non-holiday periods when it is not so crowded, Mt. Snow is a fine choice for a family.

BROMLEY, VERMONT

Bromley has always been known as a family area, and its fine nursery confirms this reputation. Also, the area is well centralized with the ski school meeting place, base lodge, ticket window, and nursery all together at the foot of the lifts. The nursery is very well equipped with large picture windows looking out on the slopes and skiers. It is run more like a school with a daily schedule of special crafts and planned activities. There is a separate crib room, kitchen and even a children's dining room. A nursery ski program for three-through six-year-olds is available, however the parents must get the children dressed and take them out to their classes which could prove somewhat of a nuisance. The instructors will return the children. On weekends and holidays, a special group of high school students is on hand at the nursery for extra supervision and outdoor play.

The area personnel is on the lookout for children and willing to help them locate Moms, Dads, ski instructors, etc. Children's classes meet at the Snoopy signs and specially trained children's instructors work with the children. For years, children have come to Bromley to learn to ski and Karl Pfeiffer and his instructors are keeping the family image alive. All day supervision is available on weekends and holidays which is a great help and fun for the kids. Bromley offers fine Vermont skiing with plenty of good slopes and a pleasant, relaxed atmosphere.

GLEN ELLEN, VERMONT

Glen Ellen was just purchased in 1975 by Harvey Clifford, and plans are underway to expand and further develop the programs and facilities. Currently Glen Ellen does not have a nursery, however the addition of one is being considered. Although there is not as great a demand for extensive children's programs at Glen Ellen, there are special children's classes.

Photo by Bill Forsyth; courtesy of Bromley Mountain

The emphasis has been on keeping classes small and manageable with five kids to one instructor. No all day supervision is available.

With a summit of 4,083 feet, the highest in the Green Mountains, Glen Ellen offers fine varied terrain. Among its thirty-six trails and slopes, is its well-known, long F.I.S. run.

I recommend Glen Ellen if the children are older and not in need of supervision or extensive junior programs or if the family plans to ski together. The atmosphere is very informal, and the area seems to be well suited for groups and clubs. Also it does not seem as overcrowded as many near-by areas.

SUGARBUSH, VERMONT

Sugarbush seems especially popular with the young, metropolitan professional group, as it offers good challenging skiing, pretty girls, and a great bar for after-ski fun.

I hesitate to recommend Sugarbush for all families but if you have only nursery age children, it is acceptable. For families with young children in ski school or skiing together, I feel there are several better near-by areas. The area doesn't seem to be planned with the family in mind as it is fairly spread out. The ski school and lift tickets are available at the Gate House at the head of the parking lot. Once you have your ticket you have to backtrack to the beginner lifts. Then the Valley House Lodge, gondola, and chair lift are up a steep hill. Parents *beware* — this hill is shared by skiers skiing down to the gondola, skiers climbing up to the lifts or lodge, and worst of all, delivery trucks which rely on speed and their horns to ascend the hill. Another safety worry especially with children is that glass from our Gondola car was missing.

Classes are available for children six years old and up but there is no special children's teaching area or all day supervision. However, there are good, wide slopes with snowmaking that are fun and very skiable for kids.

On the brighter side, the nursery and ski touring are good. The nursery, known as the Valley Day School, is located in the condominium complex so plan to let the child off before parking. Run by a real professional, Mrs. Judy Reiss, it is well equipped with separate crib rooms, a kitchen, and fun toys. My one reservation is that it could get crowded during the Holidays. Nursery ski lessons are available from a specially trained and fully certified instructor on a small hill directly behind the building, which unfortunately is not fenced off. The child either supplies his own equipment or uses the nursery's.

The ski touring center is a short distance down the road in a cozy little building where you can get homemade soup and brownies. The trails are well maintained and perfect for families.

HAYSTACK, VERMONT

Haystack is a friendly family area and small enough so your children won't get lost in the crowds. The beginner teaching area lies below the base lodge so you start out on the flat and gradually work your way down the slope. This is a great idea for children as well as beginners as they are not faced with the frustrations of climbing again and again or lift riding. It is essential, however, that they learn to stop well before descending.

Special classes are available for children four years old and up, but there is no all day supervision. Children won't accidently find themselves on expert slopes as the expert area is well separated but not too far for parents to return from. The actual mountain base with more advanced terrain is reached by taking a short ride on a "shuttle" chair lift.

The nursery has its own very well-equipped building next to the base lodge and it appears to be very professionally run with arts and crafts and planned activities.

Haystack definitely attracts its regulars, and most regular season pass holders are families. In fact, several of the instructors learned to ski in the Haystack children's classes. The area is almost their home and they are anxious to welcome new families.

STRATTON, VERMONT

Stratton seems to have a great program for every family member. In fact, I found Stratton to be one of the top areas for skiing families. It is very well planned and laid out with all the facilities in close proximity: lift tickets can be purchased at a strategically placed outdoor booth, while the near-by base lodge houses the ski school desk, rental and ski shops, and eating facilities. A short distance away, opposite the regular ski school meeting area, is the Little Cub ski school building with the day care center in the basement.

At Stratton there is a program for every member from six months through Olympic racers. The area's children's programs have been beautifully organized under ski school director Emo Heinrich and his fine supervisors.

The Stratton Mountain Day Care Center, in the basement of the Little Cub Building, is well equipped and well run, although somewhat dark since it is in a basement, there is a maximum of fifteen on a first-come basis. The Lodging Association provides a list of babysitters if the nursery is filled but I personally would like to see the nursery facilities expanded.

The Little Cub Ski School is for three- through six-year-olds. Under the direction of Muriel Burton, the pro-of-pros with nursery ski schools, the efficiently run program provides supervised activities before and after ski lessons, and lunch in a bright, cheery, well equipped building.

Ruthie Rowley and her specially trained instructors are great at teaching the six-through twleve-year-olds in the Cub Ski School. This group, ranging from beginners to racers, has available a special trail with contoured forms and cut-outs. As for racing programs, Stratton has plenty. There are classes for all interests, weekend racers to racers in full season long training and tutorial programs. No all-day supervision is available for the Cub School, but the area is centralized enough so that coming down for lunch does not pose a great problem.

Stratton Mountain certainly seems to be one of the leaders in teaching children to ski. With ten lifts, some forty trails and forty-two acres of snowmaking to assist mother nature, plenty of fine skiing is to be had.

KILLINGTON, VERMONT

Killington is a very large ski complex with several base lodges and Skye Peak, Killington Peak, Snowdown Mountain, and Rams Head Mountain. The peaks are joined by inter-connecting trails. Yet, by virtue of its size, it can be very confusing to first time visitors. A child can easily end up at the wrong lodge or worse yet, unintentionally on an expert slope. Families should head to the Snowshed Lodge for ski school, rentals, repair, and nursery.

The nursery is on the ground floor of the Snowshed Lodge, yet inconveniently paid-for upstairs at the ski school desk. It is adequately equipped but almost resembles a gym locker room. I also felt it was too hectic and too casually run, considering that children as young as two are being cared for.

Killington is known for its excellent ski school and learn-to-ski weeks aimed mostly at adults although children's classes are available. The instructors work on a rotational basis and although many are excellent, they are not specially trained to teach children. Also there is no separate children's teaching area or all-day program. With an area so large and spread out, the absence of an all-day program proves difficult. Hopefully under the supervision of Mary Douglas, the children's programs will expand and develop.

There is no doubt that, with 3,060 vertical feet of great terrain, fine skiing is to be had. Also there is plenty of fun to be had off the slopes in many local night spots.

MAD RIVER GLEN, VERMONT

Mad River Glen is so centralized, friendly, family oriented and uncommercialized that you have the feeling it is a private club. It's nursery is called the Cricket Club and is located in a separate bright, cheery building close to the base lodge. The building was built specifically for a nursery and has its own kitchen, crib rooms and large sunny windows. It is pleasant, well run and well supplied with good equipment.

The ski school, under the direction of Dixi Nohl, has set up fine programs for all ages starting with four-year-olds. The nursery staff delivers the youngest to the ski school meeting place and the instructors take them back after class. While there is currently no special children's teaching area, one is under consideration. The area sponsors many races and its excellent Junior race training program includes racing camps on a seasonal basis. In addition, NASTAR races are held Thursdays and Sundays. Mad River Glen also sponsors special races just for fun that can prove or improve your ability plus provide great pleasure. Each Monday there is a no-stop-no-fall race in which a specific trail must be negotiated without stopping or falling. On Thursday, there is the Grand Prix Downhill, and oc-casionally a marvelous family race known as the Chipmunk race. The only entry require-ment is that you can write your name.

If your family has serious and beginning skiers, this is the place. Many slopes are ex-tremely challenging and Mad River is known for the expert skiers it produces and attracts. Yet, even the beginner child will soon feel at home and confident with the excellent in-struction.

STOWE, VERMONT

Stowe, often referred to as the "ski capital of the East", is actually the name of a beautiful New England town. Three separate mountains, all under the same management,

are up the road a few miles. Unfortunately, because it is quite spread out, it is very difficult for a family of varied ski abilities. There are no nursery facilities at the mountains; nurseries and babysitting services are all located in town, for which an up-to-date list can be obtained from the Chamber of Commerce, or the Stowe Information Service.

Excellent skiing is available yet families have to do a lot of organizing and planning to take advantage of the super terrain and three mountains. The beginner area and children's "Winnie the Pooh" ski school is at Toll House. Up the road a bit, by car or shuttle bus, is Spruce Mountain (Big and Little Spruce). Spruce is mostly for intermediate and advanced skiers and probably offers the best all-around family skiing. Across from Spruce, again by car or shuttle bus, is famous Mt. Mansfield. Experts will be constantly challenged by such famous runs as "National", "Star", "Goat", "Lift Line", and "Nose Dive". Intermediate terrain is available but it is mostly an advanced skiers' mountain. Mt. Mansfield is also Vermont's highest mountain, 4,393 feet with spectacular views. The ski school under Peter Ruschp and children's director Dave Stewart does offer some excellent children's instruction. Very good young skiers meet for advanced classes at the bottom of the T-bar on Mt. Mansfield. There are no general children's classes on Mt. Mansfield unless a certain number of pupils ask for it. Mostly, good little skiers are accepted right into the adult classes. At Spruce, there is a separate children's meeting area and separate children's classes, though the child must be an intermediate skier to qualify. Freestyle and racing classes are also offered daily at Spruce.

Toll House is a fantastic place for children to learn. The ski school accepts children five years and over and its meeting area is easily recognized by the signs depicting Pooh, Kanga, Tigger, Eeyore, and other familiar friends. The children are given color coordinated labels with their names to help designate their ability or class level. With the specially trained instructors, the children are taught in a separate teaching area with a marvelous "terrain garden" or ski playground to promote learning with fun. Toll House also offers delightful adventure trails such as the "Mini-Glades" and "Woods Run". On Fridays, the children star in the Lollipop Slalom with everyone receiving prizes — yes, lollipops! When parents enroll their children in the "Winnie-the-Pooh" ski school, they are given a special pamphlet with full information plus suggestions for preparing the child for ski school and skiing which is extremely helpful.

The "Winnie-the-Pooh" ski school and regular children's classes are very well run and very professional. From my experience, if children can eventually conquer the expert trails on Mt. Mansfield, they will probably be able to ski anywhere.

With no all-day supervision program available and with an area so broadly separated, Stowe can perhaps become too difficult for some families to manage. If you are an advanced skier and your child is a beginner, you must resign yourself to a day at Toll House or bring along a neighborhood babysitter. If all members of the family are Spruce skiers, then Stowe is more manageable. Also, joining up for lunch after ski school at Spruce happens to pose no problem. Hopefully, Stowe will soon expand its programs to include all day supervision which is so essential at such a large area.

Ski touring at Stowe; photo by Frankie

CANNON-MITTERSILL, NEW HAMPSHIRE

Cannon is another ski area in the group of "Ski 93" areas. One of the first ski areas in this country, Cannon is surrounded by the beautiful high granite peaks of New Hampshire and overlooks lovely Profile Lake. It seems natural that the ski pioneers decided to build a ski area here back in 1938. The area is rich in history with many tales told of skiing adventures in the early days at Cannon Mountain. With twenty-seven miles of ski trails, there is both fun and challenging skiing to be had.

Unfortunately, Cannon is somewhat spread out with two separate base areas, one at the foot of the aerial tram way and the other at the base of the Peabody lifts. Families should head for the Peabody area. Families that avoid the tram and just ski on the chairlift slopes will find the area very manageable. The tram can prove logistically difficult for family skiing since you must remove your skis, go inside to a ticket window, show your lift pass, and get a numbered tram ticket. You then wait, on week-ends up to a half hour, till your tram number is called. Since other lifts are available, I'd suggest families avoid the tram, unless it is an uncrowded weekday.

My other concern for families skiing at Cannon is the number of "hot dog" skiers on the mountain. Since the mountain does offer challenging terrain, these fast young dare devils seem to flock to Cannon. The management tries to control this problem by revoking the lift tickets of reckless individuals and prohibiting fast skiing in certain restricted areas. However, I feel parents should be warned that the problem still exists.

The nursery is in the basement of the new lodge and unfortunately has only a few small, high windows but seemed modern and well equipped. It is only open on weekends and accepts a maximum of fifteen children. This number is a good one as the room is not extremely large. Parents must pick their children up promptly at 12:00 as the nursery closes between 12:00 and 1:00, an inconvenience, in my opinion. If the parent is held up by a lift line, getting down by 12:00 could be a problem.

Cannon Mountain is owned and operated by the state. The ski school concession is changing hands and whoever gets it will, I hope, expand the children's programs. There is no separate children's meeting or teaching area. There is a great seasonal weekend program for five- through eight-year-olds, who can already make their turns well, known as the "Teeny Wieners" which hopefully will continue next year.

My feeling is that Cannon is best suited for a family with competent skiers and a family not dependent upon organized children's programs, unless the new ski school expands and provides additional activities and facilities. However, there is definitely great skiing available at Cannon.

It is also fun to have another area right next door. Mittersill is the neighbor of Cannon and lift tickets are interchangeable. They actually share the same mountain with different exposures. Mittersill, a little resort with an Austrian flavor, is built around a hotel lodge. It has 110 acres of skiable terrain and while it appears to be a pleasant family area, the spring thaw beat me to Mittersill and they were closed when I arrived.

LOON MOUNTAIN, NEW HAMPSHIRE

Loon is nestled away in the trees on a beautiful New Hampshire mountainside with a good north-eastern exposure. A new gondola and three chair lifts wisk you rapidly up to the top to take advantage of the 100 acres of skiable terrain. The area is fairly centralized and has a relaxed family atmosphere. The ski school meeting place is not far from the base lodge complex which houses the Carol Reed Ski Shop and the rental facility, a cafeteria, a bar, and various offices including the ticket and ski school desk. However, several flights of stairs are involved which might prove a little difficult for small children in large ski boots. You climb up the stairs from the parking lot and down to the rental shop, and down to the restrooms.

The nursery however is not located in the base lodge but in the basement of the Inn at Loon. This is a short walk up the hill from the base lodge, yet it is adviseable for parents to drive to the Inn and deposit the child first before parking. The nursery has plenty of room for children to play yet it is more a babysitting service. Two girls watch the children in a large room which doubles as the Inn's recreational game room in the evening. While there are toys, by comparison it is not a well equipped nursery. Cribs are available but not separated, and the bathrooms are out of the room and down the hall. However, children do have plenty of room to run. There is no age limit, limitation of numbers, so it is a service you can count on, although somewhat lacking in facilities. Lunch is available however, so parents need not return to pick up their children.

For nursery children three through six who wish to ski, there is a good program called "Ski Mites". The instructor picks the children up from the nursery for an hour of skiing in the morning and an hour in the afternoon. The instructor then returns the children directly to the nursery. The one problem with this program is that the children have a long walk struggling with ski equipment up from the basement nursery at the Inn to the actual ski slope area. Plans are being considered to create a child's ski area closer to the nursery. The instructors are certainly very diligent and marvelous with children. Their main goal is that the children have fun and enjoy themselves in the fresh air as they become more familiar with skiing.

The ski school at Loon is very interested in children and has several special programs. Children six years old and up (although the age is flexible) are in the regular ski school. Loon has a special children's meeting area and an enclosed teaching area and plans are underway to expand and improve it. Loon also has a unique slope, "The Bear Cub Trail," which has a sign stating "Adults permitted only when accompanied by a child". This woodsy maze is a delight for many a child. The Pewee Patrol helps look for lost parents. Children's classes are offered in both the morning and afternoon, but no all day supervision is available for the regular ski school. Yet, since the area is centralized, picking children up from the ski school for lunch is fine. Loon definitely is a good family area.

WATERVILLE VALLEY, NEW HAMPSHIRE

Waterville Valley, situated in a scenic New Hampshire valley, offers the skiing family two separate mountains. Each mountain is within a short drive or shuttle bus ride from the lodging accommodations. The larger area is Mount Tecumseh. This enjoyable mountain offers 250 acres of ski terrain with a 2020 foot vertical drop which means plenty of good family skiing. If Mount Tecumseh is too crowded, nearby Snow's Mountain is opened on weekends and during the Holiday season. Ticket sales at Snow's Mountain are limited to 600 skiers, assuring short lift lines.

As I skied on Mount Tecumseh on a warm March day, there was no question that this was a children's area. In fact, I think there may well have been more children skiing than adults. The children were of all age and ability levels from three-year-old beginners to junior national racing champions. They were in ski school, with their parents, or on their own. The area is well laid out so older children who are strong skiers can manage on their own. Also, both mountains are well centralized with the base lodge at the foot of most of the lifts. Children seem to have no problem meeting up with their parents. Although Mount Tecumseh seemed to be a children's mountain, many professionals and experts were "taking the bumps" under the lift line. There is plenty of excitement and enjoyment for all levels of skiers.

Waterville Valley has two child care facilities. One facility is an infant nursery across from the ski touring center near Snow's Mountain which cares for children in diapers and infants. It is a bright and cheery room just for babies with play pens, a changing table, and infants' toys. I feel it is a good idea to have a separate area just for very young children and this nursery seemed to be very pleasant. There is no separate crib room however, so that sleeping in a noisy room may be a problem. Parents provide lunch, but the staff feeds the babies so you need not return at noon.

The Mount Tecumseh nursery is for children out of diapers, three through six years old. Located on the ground floor of the base lodge at the Mount Tecumseh area, it is well equipped with lots of toys, separate bathroom facilities, and ample craft supplies. Unfortunately, there is no limit to the number of children allowed and on a busy weekend or holiday, I can only say HELP! No lunch is provided, yet parents are able to pick up the children for lunch at their convenience. Since the area is centrally arranged, getting down to meet your child at lunch does not pose as great a problem as at some of the more expansive areas. For nursery children wishing to be introduced to skiing, an "on-ski nursery" program is available. Children supply their own equipment. The instructor picks them up at the nursery and takes them out to the beginners' hill with its own J-bar lift. She carefully instructs them and then returns them to the nursery. Unfortunately, there is no separate children's teaching slope.

For older children, a Junior Ski School with special classes is available with instructors who teach only children and are real pros. The Junior Ski School also has its own special meeting place right by the rental shop. The children's classes seem to spend a lot of time skiing and waste little time standing around talking. My one worry is that over peak periods the classes could become far too crowded, especially with the nursery skiers. Children can enroll in a one- or two-lesson day but there is no all-day supervision. All levels of skiing are offered from beginner to racing and freestyle. Children's ski week and NASTAR races are also available.

It is not unusual to read about Waterville Valley junior skiers winning freestyle championships or junior races. The area offers several fine and extensive seasonal programs in both competitive and non-competitive freestyle and racing. For those children interested in just improving their ability and pure recreational skiing, there is the Mountain Brigade. All children begin the year as privates and as they progress, they earn stripes as sergeants, lieutenants and eventually generals. There is as much emphasis on discipline and courtesy in the Mountain Brigade as there is on skiing ability. In fact, the Mountain Brigade even has its own song and lots of pride.

The demand for children's programs at Waterville Valley is very great and hopefully, under the direction of ski school director Paul Pfosi, the programs will expand and before long, children will have their own teaching area and perhaps their own slope.

BRETTON WOODS, NEW HAMPSHIRE

Bretton Woods is one of the newest areas in New Hampshire and part of the "Ski 93" group. It is nestled at the foot of Mt. Washington and offers the New Hampshire skier some breathtaking views. By comparison, it is a fairly small area; yet, it does offer fine family skiing. The Bretton Woods base lodge is, without doubt, one of the most beautiful I have seen. It is very well designed to handle skiers of all ages attractively, comfortably, and efficiently for which the architect is to be commended.

On the top level, there is a great bar with a nearby seating area surrounding an open fireplace. Here parents can sit back and enjoy an apres-ski drink. The main level offers a cafeteria with plenty of seating, the ski school and information desks. The lower level houses the ski rental shop, ski shop, rest rooms, a game room, the ski patrol room, and the nursery. The game room with many quarter-hungry machines seems to keep older children occupied while parents enjoy their hot toddies upstairs. The ski rental shop is well stocked with first rate equipment. The personnel seems very knowledgeable about fitting children with equipment, both Alpine and Nordic, and are willing to take extra time to assure that adjustments are properly made.

The nursery is also located on the lower level, but unlike most "basement" nurseries, it has lots of glass and is bright and cheery. Space is not exceedingly large but the staff has realized this and allows a maximum of only twenty children. The room is well equipped with lots of toys, craft supplies, television, and a marvelous merry-go-round powered by tricycles. The nursery accepts any age children as long as they are out of diapers. Since there is no upper age limit, an older child who does not feel quite up to skiing that day would be welcomed in the nursery. The biggest bonanza for skiing families is that the nursery is free Monday through Friday which can provide a substantial savings for the ski budget. The only drawback is that the nursery lacks separate bathroom facilities so that children must walk down the hall and share with everyone else.

Special classes are offered for children six years old and up, although the addition of a nursery ski school is under consideration. Most of the children's ski school activities take place on weekends and during holiday periods. During a normal weekday, there is neither the crowd nor the demand for special children's programs. Most younger skiers at Bretton

Woods during the week are there as part of local school programs. Children's classes *are* offered at all times but vary according to demand and ability levels of the children.

The weekend holiday program is known as "Kid's Stuff" in which there are several options. The parent can enroll the child for a half-day lesson, two half-day lessons, or a series of lessons over several successive weekends. Freestyle and racing classes are also available through the "Kid's Stuff" program. Bretton Woods does have special children's instructors, but there is no separate children's meeting or teaching area.

Because Bretton Woods is such a new area, the children's programs will undoubtedly soon be expanded as it becomes better known and developed. The area is well laid out and the terrain is most suitable for young skiers. Before long they are able to ski the entire mountain which helps to build their confidence.

Bretton Woods does limit the number of skiers they accept per day which keeps lift line waits to a minimum but does mean late arrivals may be turned away.

HUNTER MOUNTAIN, NEW YORK

Hunter really is a Mecca for skiing when the snow gods don't seem to be cooperating. Hunter has fantastic snowmaking equipment and a good mountain with beginner to expert slopes. It is very well developed with 36 trails, 13 lifts, and fine slopes, though, unfortunately, it is close enough to New York City to attract large crowds and on weekends and holidays it is really a mob scene.

The children's facilities at Hunter are quite lacking in my opinion. The nursery is best described as barely adequate in a small, poorly ventilated and ill-equipped basement room. If you have a choice, leave your child comfortably at home with a babysitter.

I also have doubts about the children's ski school. For an area that has much demand for such programs, they seem very haphazard and disinterested. My biggest concern is that children are often taught at the bottom of two very busy trails and not far from a distracting lift line. There is a beginners' area, but it is a long walk from the base lodge and often not even used for children's classes. No all-day program is available, yet getting down to meet children is not a problem. Also on the bright side, there is a fine season-long weekend program for the six- through twelve-year-old group. They meet with the same coaches and work on racing or recreational skiing under the Hunter Mountain Racing Foundation. One interesting requirement for boys to be accepted is that they have short hair.

If you are skiing with your children during the week, Hunter offers fine skiing, yet be prepared for a sizeable crowd even then since Hunter does have the best terrain and snow in the vicinity.

Ski Area Directory

The following listings should be self-explanatory except for the letter codes which are used to indicate the costs for various programs and facilities. Because costs change so regularly, it did not seem wise to do more than indicate relative prices. Therefore, the letter A indicates a cost that is higher than the average, the letter B an average cost, and the letter C, a lower than average cost. The designation A + indicates a premium high price.

I can only repeat that all of this information is based on data supplied by the areas themselves, and is very definitely subject to change. For those who want to be sure, the address and telephone number of each area is given to permit a last-minute check of any of the details that follow.

ALASKA
OREGON
WASHINGTON

	Mt. Alyeska Girdwood, Alaska 99587 (907) 783-6000	Mount Bachelor P.O. Box 828 Bend, Ore. 97701 (503) 382-2442	Mt. Hood Meadows P.O. Box 47 Mt. Hood, Ore. 97041 (503) 337-2222	Multorpor/Ski Bowl Government Camp, Ore. 97028 (503) 272-3330	Timberline Lodge Government Camp, Ore. 97028 (503) 272-3311	Crystal Mountain Crystal Mountain, Wash. 98022 (206) 663-2264 or 663-2265
NURSERY						
Daily	see below	yes[2]	no	no	yes	yes
Weekends & Holidays	see below	yes	no	no	yes	yes
Ages	see below	any	no	no	2-8 yrs.	2 yrs. & up
In diapers	see below	yes	no	no	yes	yes
Lunch	see below	?	no	no	no	no
Reservations	no	yes under 1 yr	no	no	no	no
Cost	see below	B	no	no	C	C
SPECIAL PRE-SCHOOL SKI SCHOOL						
Daily	Wed. only	no	no	no	no	no
Weekends & Holidays	yes	no	no	no	no	no
Ages	to 6 yrs.[1]	no	no	no	no	no
All day w/lunch	yes	no	no	no	no	no
Equipment incl.	yes	no	no	no	no	no
Cost	B	no	no	no	no	no
CHILDREN'S SKI SCHOOL						
Daily	yes	yes	no	no	yes	no
Weekends & Holidays	yes	yes	yes	yes	yes	yes
Ages	6-12 yrs.	6 yrs. & up	7 yrs. & up	7-12 yrs.	7-11 yrs.	5/6 yrs. & up
All day w/lunch, supervision	no	no	no	yes	no	no
Cost	C	B	[3]	[3]	B	[3]
Racing	yes	yes	yes	?	?	yes
NASTAR	no	yes	no	no	no	yes
Freestyle	yes	yes	yes	yes	?	?
SKI RENTALS						
Junior equip.	yes	yes	yes	?	yes	yes
Junior cost	C	B	A	?	B	A
SKI LIFTS						
Adult cost	A	B	B	B	B	B
Junior cost	A	B	B	B	C	B
Junior age	10 yrs. & under	12 yrs. & under	12 yrs. & under	11 yrs. & under	11 yrs. & under	12 yrs. & under
Ski Touring at area	yes	yes	yes	yes	yes	no

[1]Toilet trained   [3]Lesson packages, consecutive weeks
[2]Thurs., Fri., Sat. & Sun.

ALASKA
OREGON
WASHINGTON

	49 Degrees North Chewelan, Wash. 99109 (509) 935-6649	Mt. Baker Ski Area 2014 Moore St. Bellingham, Wash. 98225 (206) 734-6771	Stevens Pass Leavenworth, Wash. 98826 (206) 973-2500
NURSERY			
Daily	yes	no	no
Weekends & Holidays	yes	no	yes
Ages	?	no	1 yr. & up[1]
In diapers	?	no	yes
Lunch	no	no	no
Reservations	no	no	no
Cost	C	no	C
SPECIAL PRE-SCHOOL SKI SCHOOL			
Daily	no	no	yes
Weekends & Holidays	no	no	yes
Ages	no	no	8 yrs. & under
All day w/lunch	no	no	no
Equipment incl.	no	no	no
Cost	no	no	C
CHILDREN'S SKI SCHOOL			
Daily	no	yes	yes
Weekends & Holidays	yes	yes	yes
Ages	4 yrs. & up	any	8 yrs. - 14 yrs.
All day w/lunch, supervision	yes	no	no
Cost	B	C	C
Racing	yes	yes	yes
NASTAR	no	no	no
Freestyle	no	yes	no
SKI RENTALS			
Junior equip.	yes	yes	yes
Junior cost	B	A	A
SKI LIFTS			
Adult cost	B	B	B
Junior cost	B	C	B
Junior age	11 yrs. & under	10 yrs. & under	10 yrs. & under[2]
Ski Touring at area	yes	?	no

[1] Child must be walking
[2] Free kindergarten rope tow for 8 yrs. and under completely supervised and open on week-ends

Photo by Paul Meyerhoff II; courtesy of Mt. Alyeska, Alaska

CALIFORNIA NEVADA

	Alpine Meadows, P.O. Box AM, Tahoe City, Calif. 95730, (916) 583-4232	Badger Pass (Yosemite National Park), Yosemite, Calif. 95389, (209) 372-4691	Dodge Ridge, P.O. Box 513, Long Barn, Calif. 95335, (209) 965-3474	Heavenly Valley, P.O. Box 822, South Lake Tahoe, Calif. 95705, (916) 544-3429, (800) 824-3852	Homewood Ski Area, Box 165, Homewood, Calif. 95718, (916) 525-7256	Incline, Drawer AL, Incline Village, Nev. 89450, (702) 831-0251
NURSERY						
Daily	yes	yes	yes	no¹	no	no
Weekends & Holidays	yes	yes	yes	no	no	no
Ages	2-8 yrs.	3 yrs. & up	2-8 yrs.	no	no	no
In diapers	yes	no	yes	no	no	no
Lunch	yes	no	yes	no	no	no
Reservations	no	no	no	no	no	no
Cost	A	C	B	no	no	no
SPECIAL PRE-SCHOOL SKI SCHOOL						
Daily	yes	no	no	no	yes	no
Weekends & Holidays	yes	no	no	no	yes	no
Ages	4-8 yrs.	no	no	no	3-6 yrs.	no
All day w/lunch	yes	no	no	no	no	no
Equipment incl.	no	no	no	no	no	no
Cost	B	no	no	no	?	no
CHILDREN'S SKI SCHOOL						
Daily	yes	yes	yes	?	yes	yes
Weekends & Holidays	yes	yes	yes	?	yes	yes
Ages	12 yrs. & under	5 yrs. & up	12 yrs. & under	?	?	5 yrs. & up
All day w/lunch, supervision	no	no	no	?	no	no
Cost	C	?	B	?	?	B
Racing	yes	yes	yes	yes	no	yes
NASTAR	yes	yes	yes	no	no	no
Freestyle	?	no	no	yes	no	yes
SKI RENTALS						
Junior equip.	yes	yes	yes	yes	yes	yes
Junior cost	C	B	C	B	B	B
SKI LIFTS						
Adult cost	A	B	B	A	B	B
Junior cost	B	B	B	B	B	B
Junior age	7-12 yrs.²	12 yrs. & under	12 yrs. & under	12 yrs. & under	?	12 yrs. & under
Ski Touring at area	yes	no	no	no	?	yes

¹available in South Lake Tahoe
²6 yrs. and under: special low rate

CALIFORNIA NEVADA

	Kirkwood Meadows Kirkwood, Calif. 95646 (209) 258-6000	Mammoth Mountain Ski Area P.O. Box 24 Mammoth Lakes, Calif. 93546 (714) 934-2571	Northstar at Tahoe P.O. Box 129 Truckee, Calif. 95734 (916) 562-1010	Snow Valley P.O. Box 8 Running Springs, Calif. 92382 (714) 867-2434	Squaw Valley P.O. Box 2007 Olympic Valley, Calif. 95730 (916) 583-4316	Sugar Bowl Norden, Calif. 95724 (916) 426-3651
NURSERY						
Daily	no	yes	no	no	yes	no
Weekends & Holidays	yes	yes	no	no	yes	no
Ages	3-7 yrs.	2-8 yrs.	no	no	2-6 yrs.	no
In diapers	no	no	no	no	yes	no
Lunch	no	yes	no	no	yes	no
Reservations	no	yes	no	no	no	no
Cost	?	B	no	no	B	no
SPECIAL PRE-SCHOOL SKI SCHOOL						
Daily	no	no	no	no	yes	no
Weekends & Holidays	no	no	no	no	yes	no
Ages	no	no	no	no	3-5 yrs.	no
All day w/lunch	no	no	no	no	no	no
Equipment incl.	no	no	no	no	no	no
Cost	no	no	no	no	C	no
CHILDREN'S SKI SCHOOL						
Daily	yes	yes	yes	yes	yes	yes
Weekends & Holidays	yes	yes	yes	yes	yes	yes
Ages	12 yrs. & under	6-12 yrs.	6-12 yrs.	?	6-12 yrs.	5 yrs. & up
All day w/lunch, supervision	no	no	yes	no	no	no
Cost	B	B	B	C	B	B
Racing	yes	yes	yes	no	yes	yes
NASTAR	yes	no	yes	no	yes	no
Freestyle	?	yes	yes	no	?	no
SKI RENTALS						
Junior equip.	yes	yes	yes	?	yes	yes
Junior cost	B	C	B	?	A	B
SKI LIFTS						
Adult cost	A	A	A	B	A	A
Junior cost	B	B	B	B	[2]	B
Junior age	12 yrs. & under	12 yrs. & under	6-12 yrs.[1]	12 yrs. & under	12 yrs. & under	11 yrs. & under
Ski Touring at area	yes	yes	yes	no	yes	?

[1] 5 yrs. & under — free
[2] 12 yrs. & under — free when accompanied by a full paying adult

ARIZONA
NEW MEXICO
UTAH

	Sunrise McNary, Ariz. 85930 (602) 334-2122	Taos Ski Valley Taos Ski Valley, N.M. 87571 (505) 776-2266	Alta Alta, Utah 84070 (801) 742-3333	Park City Park City, Utah 84060 (801) 649-8111	Park West P.O. Box N Park City, Utah 84060 (801) 648-9871	Snowbird Snowbird, Utah 84070 (801) 742-2000
NURSERY						
Daily	yes	yes	no	yes	?	yes[3]
Weekends & Holidays	yes	yes	no	yes	yes	yes
Ages	to 7 yrs.	3-8 yrs.	no	any	3-7 yrs.	4 yrs. & up
In diapers	yes	no	no	yes	no	no
Lunch	yes	no	no	yes	yes	yes
Reservations	no	no	no	yes	no	no
Cost	B	B	no	B	B	free[3]
SPECIAL PRE-SCHOOL SKI SCHOOL						
Daily	yes	yes	no	yes	yes	no
Weekends & Holidays	yes	yes	no	yes	yes	no
Ages	4-7 yrs.	3-8 yrs.	no	3-6 yrs.	3 - 7 yrs.	no
All day w/lunch	yes	yes	no	yes	no	no
Equipment incl.	yes	yes[1]	no	no	no	no
Cost	A	A	no	B	B	no
CHILDREN'S SKI SCHOOL						
Daily	yes	yes	no[2]	yes	no[5]	yes
Weekends & Holidays	yes	yes	no	yes	yes	yes
Ages	8-13 yrs.	to 12 yrs.	no	6-12 yrs.	7-13 yrs.	4 yrs. & up
All day w/lunch, supervision	no	yes	no	yes	yes	yes
Cost	B	A	no	B	B	A
Racing	yes	yes	yes	yes	yes	yes
NASTAR	yes	yes	no	yes	no	yes
Freestyle	yes	yes	no	yes	yes	yes
SKI RENTALS						
Junior equip.	yes	yes	yes	yes	no	yes
Junior cost	B	A	?	C	no	B
SKI LIFTS						
Adult cost	B	A	C	B	B	B
Junior cost	B	B	no	B	C	[4]
Junior age	12 yrs. & under	12 yrs. & under	no	12 yrs. & under	12 yrs. & under	[4]
Ski Touring at area	yes	no	no	yes	yes	yes

[1]Strap on wood skis for small tots
[2]Children accepted in adult classes
[3]Available to Lodge guests only
[4]Chickadee Chairlift free for children 4' 4'' tall and under
[5]Available with adequate demand

Photo courtesy of Sun Valley

WYOMING
MONTANA
IDAHO

	Grand Targhee Alta, Wyo. 83422 (307) 353-2308	Jackson Hole Teton Village, Wyo. 83025 (307) 733-4005 (800) 443-6931	Big Sky Big Sky, Mont. 59716 (406) 995-4111 (800) 548-4486	Showdown Great Falls, Mont. 59403 (406) 727-5511	Bogus Basin Boise, Idaho 83702 (208) 343-1891	Sun Valley, Idaho 83353 Sun Valley, Idaho (208) 622-4111 (800) 635-8261
NURSERY						
Daily	yes	yes	yes	yes	yes	yes
Weekends & Holidays	yes	yes	yes	yes	yes	yes
Ages	any	1 yr. and up	2 yrs. & up	2 yrs. & up	2-6 yrs.	any
In diapers	yes	yes	yes	yes	yes	yes
Lunch	yes	yes	yes	no	no	yes
Reservations	no	no	no	no	no	yes
Cost	B[1]	C	A	C	C	A +
SPECIAL PRE-SCHOOL SKI SCHOOL						
Daily	yes	no	no	no	no	yes
Weekends & Holidays	yes	no	no	no	no	yes
Ages	3-6 yrs.	no	no	no	no	2-6 yrs.
All day w/lunch	no	no	no	no	no	yes
Equipment incl.	yes	no	no	no	no	no
Cost	B	no	no	no	no	A +
CHILDREN'S SKI SCHOOL						
Daily	?	yes	yes	no	no	yes
Weekends & Holidays	?	yes	yes	yes	yes	yes
Ages	?	5 yrs. & up	12 yrs. & under	2-8 yrs.	5 yrs. & up	5 yrs. & up
All day w/lunch, supervision	?	yes[2]	yes	no	no	yes
Cost	?	B	C	C	C[3]	A
Racing	yes	yes	yes	yes	yes	yes
NASTAR	no	yes	yes	no	no	yes
Freestyle	yes	yes	?	yes	yes	yes
SKI RENTALS						
Junior equip.	yes	yes	yes	yes	yes	yes
Junior cost	C	B	A	B	A	A
SKI LIFTS						
Adult cost	B	A	B	A	B	A
Junior cost	C	A	C	?	B	A
Junior age	12 yrs. & under	12 yrs. & under[4]	12 yrs. & under	?	12 yrs. & under	12 yrs. & under
Ski Touring at area	yes	yes	yes	yes	yes	yes

[1]Higher costs for children in diapers [3]Lesson packages - consecutive weeks
[2]In connection with Pooh Corner nursery [4]Eagle's Rest chairlift is free for children 12 yrs. & under

COLORADO

	A-Basin, Dillon, Colo. 80435, (303) 468-2608	Aspen Mountain, Box 4546, Aspen, Colo. 81611, (303) 925-1212 or 925-4000	Aspen Buttermilk, Box 4546, Aspen, Colo. 81611, (303) 925-1212 or 925-4000	(Aspen) Snowmass, Box 220, Snowmass, Colo. 81654, (303) 925-1220 or 923-2000	Aspen Highlands, P.O. Box T, Aspen, Colo. 81611, (303) 925-7302	Breckenridge, P.O. Box 1909, Breckenridge, Colo. 80424, (303) 453-2368
NURSERY						
Daily	yes	no[2]	no[2]	no[2]	no	yes
Weekends & Holidays	yes	no	no	no	no	yes
Ages	18 mos. & up	no	no	no	no	any
In diapers	yes	no	no	no	no	yes
Lunch	no	no	no	no	no	no
Reservations	no	no	no	no	no	no
Cost	B	no	no	no	no	B
SPECIAL PRE-SCHOOL SKI SCHOOL						
Daily	yes[1]	no	yes[3]	yes[3]	no	yes
Weekends & Holidays	yes	no	yes	yes	no	yes
Ages	4-7 yrs.	no	3-6 yrs.	3-6 yrs.	no	3-6 yrs.
All day w/lunch	no	no	yes	yes	no	no
Equipment incl.	no	no	no	no	no	no
Cost	B	no	B	B	no	B
CHILDREN'S SKI SCHOOL						
Daily	yes	no	yes	yes	yes	yes
Weekends & Holidays	yes	no	yes	yes	yes	yes
Ages	10 yrs. & under	no	6-12 yrs.	6-12 yrs.	12 yrs. & under	6 yrs. & up
All day w/lunch, supervision	no	no	yes	yes	yes	no
Cost	B	no	B	B	B	B
Racing	yes	yes	yes	yes	yes	yes
NASTAR	yes	no	yes	yes	yes	yes
Freestyle	yes	?	?	?	yes	yes
SKI RENTALS						
Junior equip.	yes	[2]	yes	yes	yes	yes
Junior cost	B	[2]	B	B	B	B
SKI LIFTS						
Adult cost	B	A	A	A	A	B
Junior cost	B	no	C	C	C	C
Junior age	12 yrs. & under	no	12 yrs. & under	12 yrs. & under	12 yrs. & under	12 yrs. & under
Ski Touring at area	yes	yes	no	yes	yes	yes

[1]If 2 or more sign up [3]Privately operated; not under Aspen Ski Corp.
[2]Available in the town

COLORADO

	Copper Mountain P.O. Box 3 Copper Mountain, Colo. 80443 (303) 668-6477	Crested Butte Ski Area Crested Butte, Colo. 81224 (303) 349-5326	Keystone Box 38 Keystone, Colo. 80435 (303) 468-1234	Lake Eidora Nederland, Colo. 80466 (303) 447-8012	Loveland P.O. Box 455 Georgetown, Colo. 80444 (303) 569-2288 or 255-7103	Powderhorn P.O. Box 1826 Grand Junction, Colo. 81501 (303) 268-5482
NURSERY						
Daily	yes	yes	yes	yes	yes	no
Weekends & Holidays	yes	yes	yes	yes	no[1]	no
Ages	18 mos.-7 yrs.	2-7 yrs.	6 mos.-9 yrs.	1 mo.-5 yrs.	1 yr. & up	no
In diapers	yes	yes	yes	yes	yes	no
Lunch	yes	yes	yes	no	no	no
Reservations	yes	no	yes - under 2 yrs.	no	no	no
Cost	B	A	A	C	C	no
SPECIAL PRE-SCHOOL SKI SCHOOL						
Daily	no	yes	yes	no	no	yes
Weekends & Holidays	no	yes	yes	no	no	yes
Ages	no	4 & 5 yrs.	3-9 yrs.	no	no	up to 5 yrs.
All day w/lunch	no	yes	yes	no	no	no
Equipment incl.	no	yes	no	no	no	no
Cost	no	B	B	no	no	C
CHILDREN'S SKI SCHOOL						
Daily	yes	yes	yes	yes	yes	yes
Weekends & Holidays	yes	yes	yes	yes	yes	yes
Ages	5-12 yrs.	6-12 yrs.	3 yrs. & up	6 yrs. & up	5-11 yrs.	5-10 yrs.
All day w/lunch, supervision	yes	no	yes - 3-9 yrs.	no	no	no
Cost	C	B	B	C	C	C
Racing	yes	yes	yes	yes	no	yes
NASTAR	yes	yes	yes	no	no	no
Freestyle	yes	?	yes	yes	no	yes
SKI RENTALS						
Junior equip.	yes	yes	yes	yes	yes	yes
Junior cost	B	A	B	C	B	B
SKI LIFTS						
Adult cost	A	A	B	B	B	B
Junior cost	C	B	C	C	C	C
Junior age	12 yrs. & under	12 yrs. & under	12 yrs. & under	12 yrs. & under	12 yrs. & under	12 yrs. & under
Ski Touring at area	yes	yes	yes	yes	no	yes

[1] Nursery expansion planned

Ski school; photo courtesy of Keystone International, Colorado

COLORADO

	Purgatory Ski Corp. Durango, Colo. 81301 P.O. Box 666 (303) 247-9000 (800) 525-5061	Steamboat P.O. Box 717 Steamboat Springs, Colo. 80477 (303) 879-0740	Telluride, Colo. 81435 (303) 728-4316 or 728-3856	Vail P.O. Box 1368 Vail, Colo. 81657 (303) 476-5677	Winter Park P.O. Box 5 Winter Park, Colo. 80482 (303) 726-5588
NURSERY					
Daily	yes	yes	yes	yes	yes
Weekends & Holidays	yes	yes	yes	yes	yes
Ages	6 mos.-8 yrs.	6 mos.-7 yrs.	6 mos.-6 yrs.	2-9 yrs.	6 mos.-8 yrs.
In diapers	yes	yes	yes	yes	yes
Lunch	yes	yes[1]	yes	yes	no
Reservations	no	no	yes[2]	no	no
Cost	A	C	A	A	B
SPECIAL PRE-SCHOOL SKI SCHOOL					
Daily	no	yes	no	yes	no
Weekends & Holidays	no	yes	no	yes	no
Ages	no	3-5 yrs.	no	2-5 yrs.	no
All day w/lunch	no	yes	no	yes	no
Equipment incl.	no	no	no	yes	no
Cost	no	A	no	B	no
CHILDREN'S SKI SCHOOL					
Daily	yes	yes	yes	yes	yes[4]
Weekends & Holidays	yes	yes	yes	yes	yes
Ages	6-12 yrs.	6-12 yrs.	4-7 yrs.	5-12 yrs.	5-12 yrs.
All day w/lunch, supervision	yes	yes	yes	yes	no
Cost	A	B	A	B	B
Racing	yes	yes	yes	yes	yes
NASTAR	no	yes	yes	yes	yes
Freestyle	yes	?	yes	?	yes
SKI RENTALS					
Junior equip.	yes	yes	yes	yes	yes
Junior cost	C	B	C	B	B
SKI LIFTS					
Adult cost	B	A	A	A	B
Junior cost	C	B	B[3]	B	C
Junior age	12 yrs. & under	12 yrs. & under	12 yrs. & under	12 yrs. & under	12 yrs. & under
Ski Touring at area	yes	yes	yes	yes	yes

[1]3 yrs. and up only   [3]5 yrs. and under, free
[2](303) 728-3575   [4]Instruction and NASTAR also available for the handicapped

Photo courtesy of Snowbird

MICHIGAN MINNESOTA WISCONSIN

	Big Powderhorn Box 136 Bessemer, Mich. 49911 (906) 932-4838	Boyne Mountain Boyne Mountain, Mich. 49713 (616) 549-2441 (312) 751-2284	Boyne Highlands Harbor Springs, Mich. 49740 (616) 526-2171	Thunder Mountain (Boyne) Boyne Falls, Mich. 49740 (616) 549-2441 (312) 751-2284	Walloon Hills Walloon Lake, Mich. 49796 (616) 549-2441 (312) 751-2284	Indianhead, Mich. Wakefield, Mich. 49968 (906) 229-5181 (800) 338-1240 or 338-1241
NURSERY						
Daily	no	yes	yes	no	no	yes
Weekends & Holidays	no	yes	yes	no	yes	yes
Ages	no	3-6 yrs.	3-6 yrs.	no	3-6 yrs.	2 yrs. & up
In diapers	no	no	no	no	no	no
Lunch	no	yes	yes	no	no	yes
Reservations	no	no	no	no	no	no
Cost	no	A	A	no	C	B
SPECIAL PRE-SCHOOL SKI SCHOOL						
Daily	no	yes	yes	no	no	no
Weekends & Holidays	no	yes	yes	no	no	no
Ages	no	3-6 yrs.	3-6 yrs.	no	no	no
All day w/lunch	no	yes	yes	no	no	no
Equipment incl.	no	no	no	no	no	no
Cost	no	B	B	no	no	no
CHILDREN'S SKI SCHOOL						
Daily	yes	yes	yes	no	no	yes
Weekends & Holidays	yes	yes	yes	yes	yes	yes
Ages	12 yrs. & under	6-12 yrs.	6-12 yrs.	6-12 yrs.	6-12 yrs.	4 yrs. & up
All day w/lunch, supervision	?	yes	yes	no	no	no
Cost	?	C	C	B	B	B
Racing	?	yes	yes	no	no	yes
NASTAR	no	yes	yes	no	no	yes
Freestyle	?	no	no	no	no	yes
SKI RENTALS						
Junior equip.	?	yes	yes	yes	yes	yes
Junior cost	?	B	B	B	B	A
SKI LIFTS						
Adult cost	B	A	A	B	B	B
Junior cost	B	B¹	B¹	B	B	B
Junior age	12 yrs. & under	12 yrs. & under	12 yrs. & under	12 yrs. & under	12 yrs. & under	12 yrs. & under
Ski Touring at area	no	yes	yes	no	no	no

¹Children under 8 yrs. ski free on beginners' rope tow

MICHIGAN
MINNESOTA
WISCONSIN

	Mount Brighton Brighton, Mich. 48116 (313) 227-1451	Lutsen Resort & Ski Area Lutsen, Minn. 55612 (218) 663-7212	Snowcrest Rt. 1, Box 272-A Somerset, Wis. 54025 (715) 247-3852	Telemark Cabel, Wis. 54821 (715) 932-4838
NURSERY				
Daily	no	no	yes	yes
Weekends & Holidays	no	no	?	yes
Ages	no	no	3-10 yrs.	to 4 yrs.
In diapers	no	no	no	yes
Lunch	no	no	?	no
Reservations	no	no	no	no
Cost	no	no	?	B
SPECIAL PRE-SCHOOL SKI SCHOOL				
Daily	no	no	yes	no
Weekends & Holidays	no	no	yes	no
Ages	no	no	4-6 yrs.	no
All day w/lunch	no	no	no	no
Equipment incl.	no	no	yes	no
Cost	no	no	C	no
CHILDREN'S SKI SCHOOL				
Daily	no	no	yes	yes[2]
Weekends & Holidays	no	no	yes	yes
Ages	no	no	6-10 yrs.	6-12 yrs.
All day w/lunch, supervision	no	no	no	yes
Cost	no	no	B	B
Racing	yes[1]	yes	yes	yes
NASTAR	yes	no	yes	yes
Freestyle	yes	?	yes	?
SKI RENTALS				
Junior equip.	yes	yes	yes	yes
Junior cost	B	A	B	C
SKI LIFTS				
Adult cost	B	B	C	B
Junior cost	no	A[3]	C	B
Junior age	no	10-17 yrs.	7-12 yrs.	12 yrs. & under
Ski Touring at area	no	yes	yes	yes

[1]Extensive Junior racing program
[2]Children's programs limited to Telemark Lodge and Townhouse guests and Telemark property owners' children. Programs also mid-week if four or more are enrolled.
[3]10 yrs. and under free

PENNSYLVANIA
WEST VIRGINIA
NORTH CAROLINA

	Camelback Tannersville, Pa. 18372 (717) 629-1661 (800) 233-8100	Jack Frost White Haven, Pa. 18661 (717) 443-8425	Snowshoe Slaty Fork, W. Va. 26291 (304) 799-6600	Beech Mountain Banner Elk, N.C. 28604
NURSERY				
Daily	yes[1]	yes	no	yes
Weekends & Holidays	yes	yes	yes	yes

NEW YORK
NEW JERSEY

	Belleayre Pine Hill, N.Y. 12465 (914) 524-5601	Catamount Hillsdale, N.Y. 12529 (518) 325-3200	Gore Mountain North Creek, N.Y. 12853 (518) 998-2523	Hunter Mountain Hunter, N.Y. 12442 (518) 263-4223	Kissing Bridge Glenwood, N.Y. 14069 (716) 592-4963	Snow Ridge Turin, N.Y. 13473 (315) 348-8456
NURSERY						
Daily	yes	yes	yes	yes	yes	yes
Weekends & Holidays	yes	yes	yes	yes	yes	yes
Ages	2-6 yrs.	1-6 yrs.	2-6 yrs.	any	any	4 wks. & up
In diapers	?	yes	?	yes	yes	yes
Lunch	no	no	no	no	yes	yes
Reservations	no	no	no	no	no	no
Cost	C	C	C	B	B	B
SPECIAL PRE-SCHOOL SKI SCHOOL						
Daily	no	yes	no	no	no	yes
Weekends & Holidays	no	yes	no	no	no	yes
Ages	no	4-7 yrs.	no	no	no	non-lift riders
All day w/lunch	no	no	no	no	no	no
Equipment incl.	no	yes	no	no	no	no
Cost	no	B	no	no	no	B
CHILDREN'S SKI SCHOOL						
Daily	no[1]	yes	yes[2]	yes	yes	yes
Weekends & Holidays	no	yes	yes[2]	yes	yes	yes
Ages	no	8 yrs. & up	5-10 yrs.	12 yrs. & under	4-11 yrs.	4 yrs. & up
All day w/lunch, supervision	no	no	no	no	no	no
Cost	no	B	C	B	C	B
Racing	yes	yes	yes	yes	yes	yes
NASTAR	no	yes	no	yes	no	yes
Freestyle	yes	yes	yes	yes	yes	?
SKI RENTALS						
Junior equip.	yes	yes	yes	yes	yes	yes
Junior cost	A	A	?	B	B	A
SKI LIFTS						
Adult cost	B	A	A	A	B	B
Junior cost	B	A	A	B[3]	A	B
Junior age	15 yrs. & under	12 yrs. & under	15 yrs. & under	12 yrs. & under	11 yrs. & under	12 yrs. & under
Ski Touring at area	yes	no	yes	no	no	yes

[1] Children accepted in regular ski school
[2] Gore handicapped ski programs also available
[3] 3 yrs. & under free

NEW YORK
NEW JERSEY

	Whiteface Mountain Wilmington, N.Y. 12997 (518) 946-2255	Willard Greenwich, N.Y. 12834 (518) 692-7337	Vernon Valley/Great Gorge Vernon, N.J. 07462 (201) 827-2000
NURSERY			
Daily	no	yes	yes
Weekends & Holidays	no	yes	yes
Ages	no	any	2-6 yrs.
In diapers	no	yes	yes
Lunch	no	no	yes
Reservations	no	no	no
Cost	no	C	C
SPECIAL PRE-SCHOOL SKI SCHOOL			
Daily	yes	no	yes
Weekends & Holidays	yes	no	yes
Ages	2-5 yrs.	no	2-6 yrs.
All day w/lunch	no	no	yes
Equipment incl.	no	no	yes
Cost	B	no	C
CHILDREN'S SKI SCHOOL			
Daily	?	no	yes
Weekends & Holidays	?	yes	yes
Ages	?	4-8 yrs.[1]	6 yrs. & up
All day w/lunch, supervision	?	no	no
Cost	?	C	B
Racing	yes	yes	yes
NASTAR	no	no	no
Freestyle	?	yes	yes
SKI RENTALS			
Junior equip.	yes	yes	yes
Junior cost	?	A	B
SKI LIFTS			
Adult cost	A	B	A
Junior cost	A	B	A +
Junior age	15 yrs. & under	12 yrs. & under	13 yrs. & under
Ski Touring at area	yes	no	no

[1]Package programs of consecutive week-ends also available for 6-18 yrs.

VERMONT
MASSACHUSETTS

	Bolton Valley, Bolton Valley, VT 85477 (802) 434-2131	Bromley Mountain, Manchester, VT 05255 (802) 824-5522	Glen Ellen, Waitsfield, VT 05673 (802) 496-3301	Haystack, Wilmington, VT 05363 (802) 464-5321	Jay Peak, Jay, VT 05859 (802) 988-2611	Killington, Killington, VT 05751 (802) 422-3333
NURSERY						
Daily	yes	yes	no	yes	yes	yes
Weekends & Holidays	yes	yes	no	yes	yes	yes
Ages	3 yrs. & up	1 mo.-7 yrs.	no	any	2-7 yrs.	2-8 yrs.
In diapers	no	yes	no	no	?	yes
Lunch	no	yes	no	no	yes	yes
Reservations	no	yes	no	no	no	no
Cost	B	B	no	B	A	A
SPECIAL PRE-SCHOOL SKI SCHOOL						
Daily	no	yes	no	no	no	no
Weekends & Holidays	no	yes	no	no	no	no
Ages	no	3-6 yrs.	no	no	no	no
All day w/lunch	no	yes	no	no	no	no
Equipment incl.	no	no	no	no	no	no
Cost	no	C	no	no	no	no
CHILDREN'S SKI SCHOOL						
Daily	yes	yes	yes	yes	yes	yes
Weekends & Holidays	yes	yes	yes	yes	yes	yes
Ages	4 yrs. & up	7-12 yrs.	14 yrs. & under	4 yrs. & up	7 yrs. & up[2]	6-12 yrs.
All day w/lunch, supervision	no	yes[1]	no	no	no	no
Cost	B	B	C	B	B	B
Racing	yes	yes	yes	yes	yes	yes
NASTAR	no	no	no	no	yes	no
Freestyle	yes	yes	yes	yes	yes	yes
SKI RENTALS						
Junior equip.	yes	yes	no	yes	yes	yes
Junior cost	A	A	no	A	A	B
SKI LIFTS						
Adult cost	B	A	A	A	A	A
Junior cost	B[3]	A[3]	A	A	B	B
Junior age	12 yrs. & under	14 yrs. & under	14 yrs. & under	14 yrs. & under	12 yrs. & under	12 yrs. & under
Ski Touring at area	yes	no	no	no	yes	yes

[1]Week-ends and holidays
[2]Under 6, private lesson only unless enough demand for a class
[3]6 yrs. and under free

Help with the T-bar at Stowe; photo by Frankie

VERMONT MASSACHUSETTS

	Mad River Glen Waitsfield, VT 05673 (802) 496-3551	Magic Mountain Londonderry, VT 05148 (802) 824-5566	Mount Snow Mount Snow, VT 05356 (802) 464-3333 (800) 451-4211	Okemo Ludlow, VT 05149 (802) 228-4041	Pico Peak Sherburne Pass Rutland, VT 05701 (802) 775-4345	Smuggler's Notch Jeffersonville, VT 05464 (802) 644-8851 (800) 451-3222
NURSERY						
Daily	yes	yes	yes	yes	yes	yes
Weekends & Holidays	yes	yes	yes	yes	yes	yes
Ages	3 wks.-10 yrs.	3 yrs. & up	2-6 yrs.	to 7 yrs.	any	6 mos.-6 yrs.
In diapers	yes	yes	yes	no	no	yes
Lunch	yes	yes	yes	no	yes	no
Reservations	no	no	no	no	no	no
Cost	A	A	B	C	B	B
SPECIAL PRE-SCHOOL SKI SCHOOL						
Daily	no	no	yes	yes	yes	yes
Weekends & Holidays	no	no	yes	yes	yes	yes
Ages	no	no	3-5 yrs.	to 7 yrs.	nursery	to 6 yrs.
All day w/lunch	no	no	yes	no	yes	no
Equipment incl.	no	no	no	no	no	no
Cost	no	no	B	C	B	B
CHILDREN'S SKI SCHOOL						
Daily	yes	yes	yes	yes	yes	yes
Weekends & Holidays	yes	yes	yes	yes	yes	yes
Ages	4-9 yrs.	any	6-14 yrs.	7-14 yrs.	any	5 yrs. & up
All day w/lunch, supervision	yes[1]	no	no	no	no	no
Cost	C	B	A	B	B	A
Racing	yes	?	yes	yes	yes	yes
NASTAR	yes	no	no	no	yes	no
Freestyle	?	yes	yes	yes	yes	yes
SKI RENTALS						
Junior equip.	yes	yes	yes	yes	yes	yes
Junior cost	C	A	A	B	B	A
SKI LIFTS						
Adult cost	A	A	A	A	A	A
Junior cost	A	A	A	A	B	A
Junior age	10 yrs. & under	13 yrs. & under	14 yrs. & under	through H.S.	14 yrs. & under	14 yrs. & under
Ski Touring at area	yes	no	yes	yes	?	yes

[1]For children registered in the nursery

VERMONT MASSACHUSETTS

	Stratton Mountain Stratton, VT 05155 (802) 297-2200 (800) 451-4261	Stowe Mt. Mansfield Co. Stowe, VT 05672 (802) 253-7311	Sugarbush Sugarbush Valley Corp. Warren, VT 05674 (802) 583-2381	Brodie Mountain New Ashford, Mass. 02137 (413) 443-4752	Jiminy Peak Hancock, Mass. 02137 (413) 738-5431	Mt. Tom Ski Area P.O. Box 1158 Holyoke, Mass. 01040 (413) 536-0416
NURSERY						
Daily	yes	no	yes	yes	yes	yes
Weekends & Holidays	yes	no	yes	yes	yes	yes
Ages	6 mos.-3½ yrs.[1]	no	6 wks.-7 yrs.	2 wks.-8 yrs.	2 yrs. & up	2-5 yrs.
In diapers	yes	no	yes	yes	?	no
Lunch	yes	no	yes	no	no	no
Reservations	no	no	no	no	no	no
Cost	A	no	B	C	C	C
SPECIAL PRE-SCHOOL SKI SCHOOL						
Daily	yes	no	yes	no	no	no
Weekends & Holidays	yes	no	yes	no	no	no
Ages	3-6 yrs.	no	to 7 yrs.	no	no	no
All day w/lunch	yes	no	yes	no	no	no
Equipment incl.	no	no	yes	no	no	no
Cost	B	no	B	no	no	no
CHILDREN'S SKI SCHOOL						
Daily	yes	yes	yes	yes	no	no
Weekends & Holidays	yes	yes	yes	yes	yes	yes
Ages	6-12 yrs.	5 yrs. & up	6 yrs. & up	12 yrs. & under	6-12 yrs.	5½-14 yrs.
All day w/lunch, supervision	no	no	no	no	no	yes[2]
Cost	B	B	B	C	C	B
Racing	yes	yes	yes	yes	yes	yes
NASTAR	yes	no	yes	no	no	no
Freestyle	yes	yes	?	yes	yes	?
SKI RENTALS						
Junior equip.	yes	yes	yes	yes	yes	yes
Junior cost	A	A	B	A	A	A
SKI LIFTS						
Adult cost	A	A	A	A	A	B
Junior cost	A	A	B	A	B	B
Junior age	14 yrs. & under	13 yrs. & under	12 yrs. & under	12 yrs. & under	12 yrs. & under	14 yrs. & under
Ski Touring at area	yes	yes	yes	yes	no	yes

[1]Limited space — first come basis
[2]All day with lunch during holiday weeks

NEW HAMPSHIRE MAINE

	Bretton Woods, N.H. 03575 Bretton Woods (603) 278-5000	Cannon Mountain Franconia, N.H. 03580 (603) 823-5563	Crotched Mountain Francestown, N.H. 03043 (603) 588-6345	Gunstock Ski Area Gilford, N.H. 03246 (603) 293-4342	Loon Mountain Lincoln, N.H. 03251 (603) 745-8111	Mittersill Franconia, N.H. 03580 (603) 823-5511
NURSERY						
Daily	yes	no	yes	yes	yes	yes
Weekends & Holidays	yes	yes	yes	yes	yes	yes
Ages	any	to 6 yrs.	5 yrs. & under	any	any	any
In diapers	no	no	yes	no	yes	yes
Lunch	yes	no	yes⁴	no	yes	yes
Reservations	no	no²	no	no	no	no
Cost	B¹	C	C	C	C	B
SPECIAL PRE-SCHOOL SKI SCHOOL						
Daily	no	no	yes	no	yes	yes
Weekends & Holidays	no	no	yes	no	yes	yes
Ages	no	no	5 yrs. & under	no	3 yrs. & up	?
All day w/lunch	no	no	no	no	no	?
Equipment incl.	no	no	no	no	no	?
Cost	no	no	B	no	B	C
CHILDREN'S SKI SCHOOL						
Daily	no	?³	yes	yes	yes	?
Weekends & Holidays	yes	?	yes	yes	yes	yes
Ages	6-12 yrs.	?	5-14 yrs.	?	3 yrs. & up	8-14 yrs.
All day w/lunch, supervision	no	?	no	no	no	no
Cost	C	?	C	B	B	B
Racing	yes	³	yes	yes	yes	yes
NASTAR	no	no	no	no	no	no
Freestyle	yes	³	?	yes	yes	?
SKI RENTALS						
Junior equip.	yes	yes	?	yes	yes	?
Junior cost	A	A	?	A	A	?
SKI LIFTS						
Adult cost	B	B	B	A	A	B
Junior cost	B	B	B⁵	B	⁶	B
Junior age	14 yrs. & under	14 yrs. & under	14 yrs. & under	12 yrs. & under	14 yrs. & under	12 yrs. & under
Ski Touring at area	yes	yes	yes	yes	yes	?

¹Monday through Friday free
²Limited space — first come basis
³New programs to be available with new ski school
⁴Parents bring child's lunch
⁵Children under 5 yrs. ski free
⁶No junior rate for all facilities, chairlifts only

NEW HAMPSHIRE MAINE

	Pats Peak P.O. Box 656 Henniker, N.H. 03242 (603) 428-3245	Sunapee Mt. Sunapee, N.H. 03772 (603) 763-2356	Waterville Valley Waterville Valley, N.H. 03223 (603) 236-8311	Wildcat Mountain Jackson, N.H. 03846 (603) 466-3326 (800) 258-8902	Saddleback Rangeley, Maine 04970 (207) 864-3380	Sugarloaf Kingfield, Maine 04747 (207) 237-2000
NURSERY						
Daily	yes	?	yes	yes	yes	yes
Weekends & Holidays	yes	?	yes	yes	yes	yes
Ages	6 mos.-5 yrs.	?	any	2-8 yrs.	2½-7 yrs.	2½ yrs. & up
In diapers	yes	?	yes	yes	yes	yes
Lunch	no	?	yes¹	no	no	no
Reservations	no	?	no	no	no	no
Cost	C	?	B	C	C	C
SPECIAL PRE-SCHOOL SKI SCHOOL						
Daily	yes	no	yes	no	yes	yes
Weekends & Holidays	yes	no	yes	no	yes	yes
Ages	4-7 yrs.	no	3-6 yrs.	no	2½-7 yrs.	3½-6 yrs.
All day w/lunch	no	no	no	no	no	no
Equipment incl.	no	no	no	no	no	no
Cost	C	no	A	no	B	B
CHILDREN'S SKI SCHOOL						
Daily	yes	yes	yes	no	yes	yes
Weekends & Holidays	yes	yes	yes	yes	yes	yes
Ages	4-14 yrs.	14 yrs. & under	4-12 yrs.	4-12 yrs.	4-7 yrs.	7 yrs. & up
All day w/lunch, supervision	no	no	no	no	no	no
Cost	C	C	A	B	C	²
Racing	yes	?	yes	yes	yes	yes
NASTAR	yes	no	yes	yes	no	yes
Freestyle	yes	?	yes	yes	yes	yes
SKI RENTALS						
Junior equip.	yes	?	yes	yes	yes	yes
Junior cost	A	?	A	B	B	A
SKI LIFTS						
Adult cost	A	B	A	A	?	A
Junior cost	B	B	A	B	B	B
Junior age	14 yrs. & under	14 yrs. & under	14 yrs. & under	14 yrs. & under	?	grade 8 & under
Ski Touring at area	no	no	yes	yes	yes	yes

¹Parents bring food for baby nursery near Snow Mountain. No lunch for older children at Mt. Tecumseh nursery
²All day lift ticket plus 1 ½ hour lesson package

CANADA

	Mont Sutton, Sutton, Quebec JOE 2KO (514) 538-2545	Mont Tremblant Lodge, Mont Tremblant, Quebec JOT 120 (819) 425-2711	Sunrise Village, P.O. Box 1515, Banff, Alberta TOL OCO (403) 762-3383	Big White, RR #3, Hall Rd., Kelowna, British Columbia VON 1BO (604) 762-0402	Silver Star Ski Area, Vernon, British Columbia (604) 542-4428	Whistler Mountain, Alta Lake, British Columbia (604) 932-5422
NURSERY						
Daily	yes	no	yes	yes	yes	no
Weekends & Holidays	yes	no	yes	yes	yes	no
Ages	2-6 yrs.	no	any	2 yrs. & up	to 8 yrs.	no
In diapers	yes	no	yes	?	no	no
Lunch	no	no	no	no	no	no
Reservations	no	no	no	no	no	no
Cost	C	no	C	C	C	no
SPECIAL PRE-SCHOOL SKI SCHOOL						
Daily	no	no	no	no	no	no
Weekends & Holidays	no	no[1]	no	no	no	no
Ages	no	no	no	no	no	no
All day w/lunch	no	no	no	no	no	no
Equipment incl.	no	no	no	no	no	no
Cost	no	no	no	no	no	no
CHILDREN'S SKI SCHOOL						
Daily	yes	yes	no	yes	yes	yes[2]
Weekends & Holidays	yes	yes	yes	yes	yes	yes[2]
Ages	5 yrs. & up	5-9 yrs.	5 yrs. & up	6-12 yrs.	4 yrs. & up	5-9 yrs.
All day w/lunch, supervision	no	yes	no	no	no	yes
Cost	C	B	B	?	B	B
Racing	yes	yes	yes	yes	yes	yes
NASTAR	no	no	no	no	no	no
Freestyle	no	yes	yes	no	yes	yes
SKI RENTALS						
Junior equip.	yes	yes	yes	yes	yes	yes
Junior cost	A	B	A	A	B	A
SKI LIFTS						
Adult cost	B	B	B	B	B	B
Junior cost	C	B	B	B	B	C
Junior age	14 yrs. & under	14 yrs. & under	12 yrs. & under	12 yrs. & under	9-12 yrs.[4]	13 yrs. & under[3]
Ski Touring at area	no	yes	yes	?	yes	yes

[1] Available with adequate demand
[2] Program may not be continued
[3] 13 yrs. and under must be accompanied by an adult on lifts
[4] 8 yrs. and under free, 9-12 yrs. junior rate